BUGIS
NIGHTS

Being the First Volume of
'The Diaries of a Western Nomad'
Largely Concerned with an
Ocean Odyssey from
Jampea Island to
Singapore

CHRIS STOWERS

EARNSHAW
BOOKS

Bugis Nights

By Chris Stowers

ISBN-13: 978-988-8769-99-5

BIOGRAPHY & AUTOBIOGRAPHY

EB183

Cover: The 'Kurnia Ilahi' moored in Wuring Bay, August 1988
Photo © Chris Stowers

Back Cover Inset: The author on Jampea island, September 1988
Photo © Fredy Ruhstaller

About the Author page: Photo © Jennie Stowers

Published in Hong Kong by Earnshaw Books Ltd.

For Mark P. Morgan (1966-2013)

'Ride on, Matey.
We'll meet up soon enough.'

And in memory of Ian J. Odell (1967-1984)

CONTENTS

Contents

"The most insecure people on earth are those who are forever playing it safe."
– **Bertrand Russell**

THE TIPPING POINT

England
December 1986

THE SKY SLUMPED over South London bruised and bewildered, a destitute sky. One that'd had the shit kicked out of it the night before. It rose unsteadily now, from puddles of piss and blood and stale beer, attempting to stitch together the hole in its aching memory. The gap I was more worried about, though, was that between the Post Office van and the Ford Granada, directly ahead. It was approaching rather too fast, but I was committed to it. If I could make it past New Cross Station while the lights were green, I'd have a clear run all the way up the Old Kent Road to Elephant and Castle—assuming I didn't slow down, of course.

I tucked in my knees and elbows and flicked down a gear. The rev-counter redlined, shooting the motorbike forward. The engine crash-bar gouged a jagged strip of paint down the Royal Mail, on one side, and my handlebar smacked into the wing mirror of the Ford, launching an explosion of splintered shards, the other. I put my head on the tank, closed my eyes, cranked open the throttle, and forced my way through. Half of Deptford high street was left stalled and hooting in my exhaust trail.

God, I love being a dispatch rider.

Mercury Couriers was a real Mickey Mouse outfit, run from an office in the rafters of a derelict barn, deep in the Erith marshes. I'd become lost when trying to find the place for my job interview, but they'd hired me, regardless. Del, the boss, spent most of his time drinking our profits away down *The Welsh*. On the plus side, I made 40p a mile, from pick-up to drop-off, cash in hand.

Popping-out like a cork from the bottleneck of traffic on Westminster Bridge I careened around Parliament Square, mentally saluted Winston on his pedestal, and barreled up Whitehall, coming to a screeching halt at the steps of Admiralty House. Leaving the bike on the pavement, oil dripping from its sump and exhaust pipes clicking as they began to cool and contract, I dashed into the echoing chamber of the most hallowed of British institutes.

An aged porter peered up from his desk, scrutinizing my appearance—my battered leather jacket and rakish white silk scarf possibly put him in mind of earlier tarpaulin-clad naval heroes and privateers, those whose portraits stared down from the colonnaded walls. The patched denim jeans and scuffed knee-length boots perhaps less so; and then my hair, released from its helmeted prison, rocketing in all directions, like a direct hit on a firework factory—I feared he was going to call security. Instead, he asked without any apparent trace of concern:

"You've come for the charts, Laddie?"

Purpose and destination secured, along with a powerful company motorcycle (even if it was a junkyard Honda CX500), and the impregnable optimism native to any nineteen-year-old enjoying the novelty of first employment, I zoomed back out of London down the A2. The miles ticked profitably by ... 9.20 ... 9.60 ... £10 ...

My mission was to reach the *MV Salamander*, a five-thousand-ton merchant ship, before the tide turned. She was currently moored off the Isle of Grain, and couldn't set sail without the navigational documents in the satchel flapping wildly in my wake.

I turned off the dual carriageway, entering a sodden desolation, where ancient forts slowly subsided as awaiting the call to once again defend the estuaries of the Thames and Medway rivers from foreign invasion. I rode to the very edge of this flat earth: down the long dirt track towards an unbroken line of brown and green. Grey suggested the sky, and, looming larger, the lead red hull of a massive cargo vessel rose like a block of flats. Something permanent, but with ballast in place of foundations. It was hard not to be impressed: all of *this*, and it couldn't leave without *me*.

I clanked aboard up a steep metal staircase and handed The Admiralty's collection of maps and tide charts to a grateful navigator.

"Wish I could come with you," a desire I'd been hitherto only mildly aware of suddenly surfaced; to leave it all behind, sail away, seek my fortune elsewhere.

"Bring your passport next time and I'll see what we can do," the captain joked, waving me back down to where my motorcycle sat gently simmering on the mudflats.

The Mercury radio-pager beeped on my belt. I pulled in to a Little Chef café to call Del from its payphone. Another job. But my heart wasn't in it: I should have been aboard the *Salamander*, heading out into the English Channel. But I'd let that chance slip away. In a foul mood I punished the Honda, riding flat out, 100mph all the way. Cars flashed past in a blur, and then one pulled out and started racing me. Thinking I'd lose him at the Bexleyheath turn off, I exited the main road. He stayed on my tail. Across the roundabout and up the hill I flew, heading towards the crowded high street. I couldn't shake him. Somewhere there was a siren, and the car behind was flashing its headlights. I slowed slightly and waved at him to pass: "Go on then, overtake, you impatient bugger ..."

The driver accelerated and then swerved, forcing me to the curb. Shit. The Police.

"You do realize you were doing eighty miles per hour in a thirty speed limit—*Sir?*" The forced civility oozed from that last resentful syllable, like the congealed grease in a bag of chips.

"I was trying to get out of your way," I started to make my case, and then bit my tongue; it was probably unwise to pursue the fair and logical argument that, had he been driving an honestly marked police car *in the first place,* I would never have risked overtaking him. This was entrapment. I begrudgingly accepted the ticket, the three points on my license, and then the pager started beeping again. I removed its batteries.

"Wotcha," my best friend Mark greeted me. He was dispatching, too, out of Chichester, on England's south coast. We met for lunch, as usual, in Lincoln's Inn Fields. It was our favorite spot in all of London. The huge square was cloistered by elegant, redbrick law offices whose occupants stared disapprovingly down long noses through tall windows at the incongruous mess of homeless people living in cardboard boxes in their midst.

I ordered the usual salami sandwich and a coffee from the Italian deli on the corner. We were lucky to find an unoccupied bench. Impervious in our all-weather biking gear to the icy drizzle, we plonked ourselves down on its damp wooden surface, and I began to tell Mark of my earlier revelation on the deck of the *Salamander*:

"We have *got* to buy a boat. Doesn't need to be a big one. Something with sails, though." It was a dream we'd spent long hours discussing and embellishing.

"Or we could steal one. You can just row alongside in the night. I've seen them moored down in Chichester harbor. No security," Mark said, introducing a promising new prospect. "Wherever we sail to has got to be better than ending up here." He gestured with his coffee cup at a nearby down-and-out slumped in a pool of vomit.

"You know, at night I can see this place from home—the whole of London—it's a huge glow in the sky. Even from thirty miles away. Burning with promise," I said. "But close up ... well it's just as dirty and desperate as we are."

"It's like those bonfires Cornish ship wreckers used to light. You know, to lure boats onto the rocks? The Financial District. It's a beacon, tempting us in, waiting to strip us of our souls," Mark surprised me with his darker assessment. "Society only survives by churning through more and more people like you and me. They need us. How else can they keep the suburbs expanding, destroying all the woodland with poxy housing estates? They rely on us to breed new generations of taxpayers and consumers: people to holiday in Ibiza or Greece, who'll never dare vote for anyone too radical, and who will die obediently a few years after retirement without burdening the NHS. What's the point of it all?" And then he plotted a complete tangent:

"Those poor lads in Afghanistan are sure getting clobbered by the Ruskies."

"Can't say I'm too well up on foreign affairs, Mate," I responded. "Landlocked country, isn't it? We can't sail there. Besides, do you know any Afghans?"

"Of course not, but it's the principle of the thing. Bloody commies." And he retreated into some distant mental sanctuary. "Been meaning to tell you," he mumbled after a long moment contemplating his boots. "I'm joining the army."

Silence fell along with a first dusting of snow, muting the pleas of panhandlers and pausing the traffic in disarray. I was stung with disappointment:

"So, no sailing away, then …?"

"No. Sorry, Matey. It's now or never. We can meet up in all those foreign parts I'll be posted to, when I get leave. It'll be great!"

Mark raised his arm in farewell and rode off, his bike describing unsteady black snakes through the greying slush. Alone again, I experienced a sudden, unexpected wave of …. *relief.* He must have been wrestling with his conscience a long time, and even now I sensed was not completely sold on the idea of the military. But he was too proud and stubborn to back out. And I possessed no compelling argument to mount against his logic. He had been brave enough to tell me to my face at least, and now I was free to set out on my own path, too.

To that end, I've a confession to make: I'd had my passport with me the whole time. I just needed a sufficiently violent nudge to do something with it.

The only thing that matches my love of England is the continuous urge I feel to get away from the bloody place. This isn't as contradictory as it might at first sound, and I know a great many of my compatriots feel as conflicted as do I. On the one hand, we are proud that the very best of our traits, attitudes and expectations are contained within the soft and cuddly bounds of a single adjective, *'mild'*. Our climate, geography, food and beer: *mild.* Our religious convictions, racial prejudices, sexual preferences, political beliefs, judicial rulings and performance in all international team sporting events since 1966: predictable, boring, but more than anything, *mild.* By instinct we steer clear of extremist views and feel faintly embarrassed for those who

8

exercise them.

At the same time, it's impossible to deny being descendants of a restless island tribe. The curious and the haunted amongst us have always gravitated like rivers to the sea, drawn by that gently warming haze beyond the horizon. From Richard the Lionheart to Livingstone and Lawrence (T.E. not D.H., of course), through the exploits and discoveries of Darwin, Drake, Cook and Wolfe, to Wellington, Nelson, Nightingale, Rhodes and Kipling – our roll call of national heroes is endless. Even the fictional ones – the Biggles's and Bonds – their reputations were all cemented *overseas*. Hell, even The Beatles, the *mildest* pop band ever, had to venture to India before their music became interesting.

We just come back home to die.

That morning, on the *Salamander*, I'd opted for 'mild'. Fearing the captain would laugh at me, think me naïve, I'd kept my passport in my pocket and my dreams to myself. But I should have had the guts to *try*. That's what was eating away at me as I'd blasted carelessly back to London, an hour later. Sixty long minutes, during which time my run-in with the law, and Mark's abandonment of our plans seemed to have flipped some internal switch. Energized by a deep-seated sense of injustice, I throttled-up the Honda. The twin cylinders stuttered reluctantly to life, choking out plumes of oily smoke. I pointed the bike out the park, and slalomed down a slippery Kingsway in the direction of the High Commission of India.

I hadn't told anyone, but for the past month I'd been in correspondence with an NGO based in Delhi and run by Jains – people so harmless they wore facial masks to avoid the accidental murder of insects. My intention to volunteer with them in the slums of their capital – along with the usual dose of tourism – I marked in the appropriate section of the visa application form.

But this innocent declaration seemed to have raised the wrath of the consular official on the opposite side of the glass. Or perhaps he was just offended by my greasy jacket and unkempt beard. Be that as it may, the bureaucrat concerned, a certain Hari Singh, made a show of branding my virgin passport with the inky initials 'VAF' — Visa Application Forwarded.

India didn't want me.

Back out on The Strand, snow was falling heavily. Fluffy clusters settled on the Honda. The ungainly machine leaned over sharply on its side-stand, resembling a shabby old tramp burdened with shopping bags, and using a walking stick to probe for support. I felt a sudden kinship with the old workhorse. Maybe I had to accept that my future, too, would never amount to anything glamorous or rise above the usual, unrelenting daily grind? I'd never breakout from England's powerful force field now. After all, there was a certain freedom that accompanied a life bereft of ambition. And there were worse fates than being assigned to an eternity of 'mildness'. Prompted by some distant reverberation of duty, I replaced the batteries in the radio-pager. It started beeping furiously.

"Where the bloody 'ell've you been?" Del abused me, after I'd finally located a box with a functioning telephone inside it. One that had a workable receiver, that hadn't been ripped off the wall, and was blessed with a coin-slot free of chewing gum and unraveled paperclips. It still smelled like a pub toilet, of course.

"Been beeping you for hours," the controller exaggerated, "Rush job. Pick up from Slough, to Bromley. Like *yesterday!*" He recited the address of a generic industrial estate, and I meekly complied. This was obviously my punishment for not having had the initiative to jump ship when earlier presented the opportunity.

And so, to Slough.

I rode down the M4 consumed in a blinding zinc blizzard. My fingers felt like they were being fed through a meat grinder, until blissful numbness took over. To guard against blacking out completely, I devised a rousing verse, and repeated it over and over at the top of my voice:

I've always wanted to get out into the world.
I don't want to miss a jot.
I thought everyone else was the same as me.
Now I know they're not.
Probably that's a good thing.

"Bike for Bromley!" I announced, staggering into the warehouse like a yeti. I signed a form, and was handed in return two mysterious, unmarked, bulky wooden crates. My frozen fingers fumbled to secure these to the pillion seat by means of straining bungee cords. I sighed, fogging up my visor completely, and plunged back into the storm. These had better be Top Secret components, vital to National Security that I'm heroically transporting at risk to life and limb ...

Turned out they were a couple of magnums of Moët. Company Christmas party in Bromley South, for the enjoyment of. Bunch of big shoulder padded, fat expense account, loud-mouthed, wide suspender-wearing Yuppie solicitors. As I sat in their waiting room, sounds of yuletide merriment leaked through the wall. I made sure to drip liberally on their carpet. A member of the decadent species eventually emerged: "Oh, didn't know you were still there, chum. That the champers?" He flashily pulled out a fistful of notes, raising my hopes of a tip: "Sorry, don't have any small change." And he'd whisked the bottles away.

That did it. I put a call through to Mercury:

"Del? Chris. I quit!"

BUGIS NIGHTS

I was getting out of this country, and any form of transportation would do. Inspired, I rushed to the travel agent on Bromley High Street just before closing time, and asked for the cheapest ticket they had to the destination closest to India. £160 was the price, for a one-way ticket to Karachi ...

"The trouble about journeys nowadays is that they are easy to make but difficult to justify."
— **Peter Fleming** (*News from Tartary*)

PART
1

A NEW BEGINNING
Kupang, West Timor, Indonesia
Wednesday, 24th August 1988

THE AIRPORT ARRIVALS hut floated on a distant shimmering lake of heat. I approached it across a vibrating chorus-carpet of cicadas, turbo props shocking the air from my lungs. A trail of sweat pursued me across the dazzling dirt landing strip. It was instantly absorbed into Asia.

"Hello meesterrrrr!" The immigration official ambushed me with a spray of 'r's like bullets from a wayward AK47. And yet his tone was friendly enough. It's nice to feel welcomed. A few steps past his desk, and another unexpected encounter:

"Chris? What are ze chances?"

Charly! I hadn't spotted him on the plane during our short flight from Darwin. What is it about chance encounters? I was beginning to suspect there was nothing 'chance' about them at all, as though the Universe had it all mapped out and the best we could do was buckle up for the ride. We immediately started chatting where we'd left off, as casually and naturally as upon our first meeting in Tibet almost exactly a year ago. Coincidence is just destiny in disguise.

The Frenchman introduced me to a new traveling mate, a long-haired and introspective German hippie, who went by the name inherited during his travels in India, 'Sabji'.

Indonesia is a majority Muslim country, but Timor was part of the Catholic Portuguese empire for hundreds of years, and plenty of churches occupied prominent positions around its capital, Kupang. Women swayed by, their hair flowing freely; and pork and beer, though relatively expensive, were consumed without guilt. Apparently, the whole east of the island was off-limits. The Indonesian army had been fighting Fretilin independence guerillas out there since 1975, but in Kupang there were no signs of conflict. It was so sultry and humid I couldn't imagine anyone summoning the energy for violence.

The sun set on the waterfront. Crowds massed around resolute chess players, offering advice, cheering the astute move; the air was permeated by the sweet tang of their *kreteks*, clove cigarettes sold singly by barefooted child vendors. Stalls lit by paraffin lamp tempted with the sizzle of *saté* and the metallic, nasal burn of chili powder carried on the smoke. A local lad offered us flakes of fried fish to try, another passed around *tuak*, a sweet and potent palm wine, which we sipped from a sculpted leaf. Much amusement arose when Charly started choking on his first swig of this local hooch.

In the West you have to pay to get a piece of the action. In Indonesia, it would appear, life was on the streets and in your face, and wealth existed to insulate you from it. Everybody was asking us questions and some inquisitively stroked the hair on our arms and legs, a naïve and curious gesture, they having none. A teenager brought out a four-string guitar: Sabji could play, being classically trained. He strummed out a few Beatles numbers and then The Rolling Stones' 'Angie', and everyone sang along.

The local motorcycle policeman came to investigate. We used his crash helmet as a drum.

CLAUDIA

MEETING CHARLY LIKE this brought memories of last year flooding back. Of Tibet, and *Her*. Claudia. You can tell within the first minute of meeting whether someone is destined to become a part of your life story, or just another ship, passing in the night. And it will be some random, insignificant, infuriating thing: the way she laughs at your joke — or doesn't laugh at your reasons for having left home — but mostly it'll be something petty, like the strands of blonde hair getting caught in her long lashes, making you want to reach out and restore order. Above this, though, is the sense of having known each other in some previous existence, maybe in a dream. And you just gravitate. None of the inhibitions or social expectations that usually get in the way, no shyness at initial contact, since there's nothing initial to any of this at all. That she's ten years older than you isn't an issue: one has to start somewhere — and after all, when you're twenty, it is statistically inevitable you'll be the younger.

"Hi, I'm Chris."

"Yes," she'd replied. That was all. And she'd shifted slightly, offering me a shoulder on which to lay my head, before retreating into her intense study of the passing scenery. The bus had arrived late, pushing through a monotony of desert, and we'd stumbled into the only hostel in town permitted to host foreigners. Odd concept, 'foreigner' — all this time I'd imagined myself being surrounded by *them*. Due to the convention of 'Beijing Time' the sky was still light at midnight this far in the west. 'Golmud', I'd thought: even the town's name is a rejection of romance.

Early in the 20th century, the British-Hungarian archeologist Sir Aurel Stein crisscrossed this region, noting how little it differed from descriptions penned by the Buddhist monk Xuanzang, in his *'Journey to the West'*, thirteen centuries earlier. The polyglot explorer was the sort of Man's Man who'd casually translate several dozen verses of the 12th century Sanskrit epic *Rajatarangini* over breakfast, and then pop out to bag a snow leopard in a blizzard. On his way he'd perhaps discover a cave complex containing ancient Buddhist manuscripts, before returning to base-camp in time for tea and to amputate a niggling, frost bitten toe or two with a serrated bayonet.

He'd be disappointed at what they've done with the place since. Ancient intrigue had been replaced by faded red communist stars clinging to cracked concrete door mantles, and loudspeakers reverberating the day's officially approved news across a vacancy of low rooftops. Beaten down by the tempest of dust, grit and coal soot that blasts unchecked across the high-altitude Qinghai Plateau from Tibet, the town exists in suspense; a squat, spindly sandcastle, wary of the next tide.

Stranded in this alien territory I'd sought comfort in the familiar. That pair of big Bavarian eyes, for instance, with long, long lashes resembling reeds surrounding twin green pools. She'd lifted her head and I'd stared deep in reflective waters, uncertain if their momentary flutter signaled encouragement or submission, or were just an involuntary reaction to the strong wind that had whipped-up suddenly from out of the desert void.

Would it be so wrong—we're in the middle of nowhere, after all—to try to kiss those eyes? Something stirred from within, a buried monster, rising, filling the air with gritty particles, wrenching its giant limbs from out of earthly interment. Claudia gripped my arm. She forced me behind a wall, just in time for us to avoid decapitation by a flying sheet of tin roofing. Gasping for oxygen, my mouth instead filled with dirt. Sandstorms are emotionally violent, and very sudden things.

"Idiot boy," she'd grinned at the birth of our intimacy. Claudia stood back, shaking the desert out of her thick mop of hair, and unfurled the scarf she'd used to cover her face during the storm. I coughed and spat out a mouthful of mud.

"Here." She poured water from her canteen over my head, jumping back, laughing. Caught up in the moment, I grabbed the container from her hand and chased her out into the main street. My boots sank deep in a pocket of sand and I stumbled and fell.

"That serves you right." She came to stand over me, and gloat. Just as suddenly, though, she relented and flopped down beside me and pressed her gravelly lips to mine. With her golden tresses entangled in my fingers I lost any urge to restore order.

KUPANG

WEALTH IS TRULY relative. I cashed a £50 traveler's check, and received 140,000 Indonesian Rupiah in a stack of grubby notes, three-inches thick. I may have had less than £400 to my name, but I was a millionaire here in Kupang. Enjoying the oddly flush sensation that only a fistful of dirty cash can truly provide, I took a stroll along the city's whitewashed streets. There were no beggars here. People were sufficiently clothed and fed, and faced none of the stark privations I'd witnessed earlier in my travels, in Pakistan and Tibet. Perhaps it was the weather. It was too hot to bother with thoughts of work or rebellion, even shelter. People called out from beneath the shade of broad trees, and time passed in noisy slurps of sweet coffee, and the measured crackling burn of a *kretek*. This was poverty with a smile; poverty that didn't know it was poor.

I boarded the night ferry with Charly and Sabji. We headed west, fourteen hours to Flores, the next island in the chain. The next morning, I was up on deck before sunrise. Sabji was already there, wrapped in his blanket, gazing at a pod of dolphins swimming parallel to us, flaunting their freedom in arcing, silvery leaps. The seas churned and a huge whale cut in front of our ship, blasting water out of its spout.

Volcanoes rose on the horizon, shadowy pyramids anchored deep below to the ocean floor. At the base of one of these, the tiny port of Larantuka slowly congealed through the tropical haze, its collection of brick and thatch matchbox houses fronted by a slender belt of swaying palms. Their trunks were like drinking straws, sucking white the sandy shore.

We found refuge in a cheap guesthouse, its rooms separated by patchy bamboo walls. It was only 7 a.m. but already I was sweating profusely and in need of a shower, or *mandi* as it was known here — the word was used as both noun and adjective — every toilet had one; a tiled tank in the corner. This was filled from a single cold-water source, and had a drainage hole at the base plugged by a huge cork. One scooped the brackish water by means of the long-handled plastic bowl that invariably floated on the surface, and squatted, braced in anticipation of the initial frigid dousing. It was the only way to keep cool.

At the far end of Larantuka's beach, a submerged coral shelf extended out to sea. In it was sustained a landscape of miniature coves and channels alive with bubble fish that swelled to three times their size when scooped out of the water, sea urchins that sprayed a sticky, white jet when disturbed, and vivid blue starfish.

Forget new beginnings. This place was like a new *planet*!

A MEETING IN MAUMERE

THE FOUR-HOUR bus ride from Larantuka to Maumere ended up taking twice as long. "*Jam karet!*" grinned the teenage bus conductor, seated in the open door well. 'Rubber time'. Indonesia ran on it. The country teemed with life, both human and botanic. I was comforted by spontaneous smiles and ritual generosity, soothed by the symphony of a language as yet unintelligible but intimate as birdsong.

Upon arrival in Maumere we searched for a café, pushing through the evening shadows towards a small market near the mouth of the creek. A quick scan of the refreshment establishments on offer forced us to lower our expectations a notch or two, and we stumbled into a *warung*, the local equivalent. I pulled out a splintered wooden bench, its legs wobbling on the uneven dirt floor as we sat down heavily, brushing off the dust of the road. A rich aroma engulfed us, spiriting our exhaustion away.

"Coffee, *mon brave*," said Charly. "Remember when we were traveling through Tibet? 'Ow we would kill for eet?" I nodded in recollection of our shared Himalayan hardships, as the thick, oily liquid was poured from a blackened kettle into short glasses spooned fully one-third deep with sugar.

Just then three westerners entered, thrusting aside the plastic drape that hung in place of a door. They had about them the appearance of determination. No mere wanderers, these. This far from home, encounters with fellow Europeans were few and often significant, so we asked them to join us.

Pascal was a rogue, a natural leader of the pack. Only twenty-eight, but looking several years older, he had tight curly hair and was possessed of incredible restless energy. It was as if he were walking on coals – were he to stop moving or talking, he'd go up in flames. Possibly looking to accelerate the process, he sparked a Marlboro. Squinting against a harsh beam of lamplight, thrown up from a pool of spilt water, he tossed the pack onto the table for general consumption.

"We are buying a ship off the Bugis," he stated.

The Bugis are famed sea-traders and pirates, rulers of the waters between their South Sulawesi homeland, Makassar, and Maumere, on Flores. They are modern-day corsairs, more at home on the deck of a tilting teak ship than they are on dry land.

During the 18th and 19th centuries, intrepid Bugis raiders plagued the trading ships of the British and Dutch East India Companies. The Bugis (pronounced 'boogy') are popularly rumored to be the origin of the saying brought back by European sailors to spice up the bedtime stories they'd tell their children, 'the bogey men are out to get you.'

The Bugis are now predominantly Muslim, having converted to Islam from their ancient animist beliefs in the 17th century to ensure their relevance in a region increasingly becoming dominated by Arabic trade.

"We've come from their home island on one of these boats, and we already paid the headman part of the money for it," joined in

Franck, just twenty years old, a co-sponsor of the venture.

"Oui, and we will sail this ship back to France in time for the bicentennial celebrations of La Republic, next year!" Pascal assured us and everyone else within shouting distance.

The third Frenchman in the group was not French at all, but Swiss. Fredy was willowy and tall with cropped blond hair, and he was a few years older than me. He was hoping to get out of Indonesia before his visa expired in two weeks' time, and attaching himself to this mad venture had offered the best chance.

I asked Franck, "What's the island? Is it far from here?"

"It is called Jampea. I doubt it will be on your map. It has no electricity or telephones ... with the wind behind you then it is ..."

"Paradise!" Fredy interrupted, eyes half-closed in pleasant recollection.

"... two days away," continued Franck. "We sailed from there with the Bugis crew, and now are stuck waiting for the rest of our team to arrive from France. They have with them the remainder of the money."

"And the video camera," added Pascal, who was intent on making a documentary out of the whole adventure. "They flew into Thailand ten days ago, but since then? *Peuf!*" he gestured, sending his fingers, as well as a pillar of cigarette ash, flying in the multiple directions of his frustrated hope.

LINGERING IN LHASA

I FOUND MYSELF powerless to resist Claudia's joyful invitation. "Let's ride!" she'd chirped, and we pedaled our heavy *Flying Pigeon* bicycles, the wind at our backs, out of Lhasa towards the sky burial site. She was dressed now not in travelers' fatigues, but in a light, floral cotton dress. Having spent the last five months in conservative Islamic Pakistan, such feminine attire worn so casually was startling to my eyes. I was happy to drink up the view, though, cycling behind her and into the sun: bright yellow sunflowers riding up her tanned thighs, her pert torso perfectly silhouetted through the garments' thinly woven mesh. Her halo of tossed straw hair filled me with more religion than a thousand smoky shrines. And those little white ankle socks that *all* German girls wear … they made my head spin.

Our route ended in death and decay. Pausing to catch our breaths in the thin air, as the dirt track steepened, Claudia handed me her compact Minolta binoculars:

"Take a look, there. See?" She guided my hands.

About a half a mile away, I could make out a shadowy corpse laid out upon a reddened stone, and ranks of attentive undertakers standing to attention at a respectful distance;

vultures waiting to carry away and consume the defunct body, once it had been hacked to pieces by a human attendant. Was this all we came down to: a takeaway for lazy predators?

As we set off, a burly Tibetan sentinel appeared out of nowhere and blocked our forward progress. Obligingly, we made a U-turn and rode on north to the largely deserted monastery at Sera, about a mile away, instead. Having eaten yogurt from glass jars sold by a local vendor at the sleepy entrance, we left our bikes in the shade of a walnut tree and began the steep climb up cobbled streets to the four-storey *Tsokchen*, the Great Assembly Hall. Before entering this, we were requested to kneel before a wiry old lama who pounded our backs with a smoothed rock. The assembled onlookers, and the old monk himself, all giggled at this obscure ritual.

From Sera we rode west along the river, a gurgling tributary punctuated by small grassy islands. Leaning our bikes together at one such islet, we went to lie in the long, soft pasture midstream; the air crystal clear and silent, bar the stereophonic burble of icy water, and buzzing of bees. The scent of honey, wildflowers and faint hint of drifting wood smoke will forever remind me of Claudia and of detachment from the rest of the world. I read some poetry and began to write postcards, but couldn't concentrate: communication beyond this enchanted glade suddenly seemed pointless. We both realized we were finally together, alone.

"Why Tibet, why now?" Claudia mused.

"India wouldn't give me a visa. I have to go around," I'd replied. A moment burbled and buzzed by.

"You know, Chris, you are so fortunate," she continued, "you have set out on the way of the world at a tender age. I very much doubt you have anything in England that you regret leaving behind?"

She was right, of course: all I owned of any worth was right with me in my backpack. There was nothing and no-one calling me back. I was unhobbled by melancholia, free to grab at all the world had on offer. There was no job awaiting my return, or family with demands on my resources and attentions. I was not on the run from debt collectors.

"I'm a clean slate, I guess you'd say: just waiting to get written on," I stared into those entrancing eyes, significantly. "And you?"

She'd laughed; maybe my face betrayed a hint of disappointment. *She's not taking me seriously*, I thought.

"I'm sorry, it's just that not all of us have such unblemished backgrounds. We mostly carry around a lot of baggage, having waited a bit too long to leave our comfort zones. I guess I'm here to try and forget ... yes, that would be the simplest way to answer your question. Let's keep it at that, for now?"

No more enlightened than earlier, I plucked a thick blade of grass, turned back absent-mindedly to my W.H. Auden, and decided that Claudia's air of mysterious regret rather suited her.

"Do you love anybody, Chris?" Claudia said later, disturbing the silence that had settled like the pollen between us.

"Well, my parents and sister, obviously ..." I began to chew on the grass stem and give the matter some thought: "... but, then, that's to be expected. Love by default."

"Idiot boy. You know what I mean."

"Then, 'no', to be blunt. I never stick around long enough, or I get bored. I prefer to be on the move, everything makes more sense in motion." Truth be told, I had no experience of this game, at all.

"Ah, there *is* a philosopher hidden in there, somewhere!" She turned on one side to face me, and started nibbling down the end of my grass stem until our mouths met halfway in a healthy, herbal kiss. *This love game seems simple enough. It's like Nature: probe for weaknesses; fill any gaps.*

I let my hand glide across the pleated floral terrain covering her hips and inch toward the firm upland flesh of a smooth, hairless thigh. A wanderer in tribal territories, it was expectant of the reception it would receive upon arrival at the white borderline of her panties. My probing prompted a shot across the bow.

"I am in love, you know?" From her tone I could tell she didn't mean with me. "And he ... well, I am pretty sure he is in love with me, too."

"Which would explain why you are here, I suppose." I mentioned a bit stuffily, my fingers retreating to the neutral territory of her waistband, awaiting further instruction.

"Yes, well, how could he explain travelling alone to Tibet to his wife?"

I tried not to act surprised. I'm a Man of the World now, after all: "So I guess purely living for the moment is out of the question?"

"That's the thing about love, idiot boy, it isn't frivolous. That's how you know it's real," she'd said, rolling over to rest on her stomach, small bulges forming where her breasts pushed into the mattress of meadow flowers, "you'll find that out for yourself, one of these days."

"You make it sound like an odious duty. I'd have thought falling in love was simple. Like falling out of a tree. Something gravitational," I said.

I'd thought that's what we had.

"Well, there's something about you ... it may take a long time for you to find love. I sense you prefer to run from it, though, and anything else that holds you to one particular place or person. You are scared to be vulnerable." That had cut right through me, as a non-admitted truth delivered by a cherished source surely must. I was saved from having to respond when Claudia turned

31

back to me and guided my head gently toward her warm bosom, the most natural harbor of atonement.

"And yet, you are a listener. You are patient," I concentrated on the beat of her heart as she muttered, stroking my hair, "you will find women are attracted to that. We can't help it. It's maddening!" she sighed. But I sensed she was smiling, too.

I'm glad I'm not the only one confused by all this.

KURNIA ILAHI

THE ISLAND OF Flores is situated closer to the sandy wastes of Australia's Northern Territory than to its own national capital, Jakarta. The principal settlement along its empty and jagged northern shore was Maumere, where Charly and I had first encountered the French, and thoughts of seaborne adventure were aroused. This morning Pascal invited me to the coastal village of Wuring, a further two miles out of town. I approached the fishing hamlet, my feet crunching along a short track of compacted sand, crushed coral, and seashells. At anchor here, floating on a shimmering mirage, was their ship, the *Kurnia Ilahi*.

"The Bugis are Muslim, that is why their village is located outside of Christian Maumere," said Franck. Although Indonesia officially sanctions five State religions (in 1988 these were Islam, Protestantism, Catholicism, Hinduism and Buddhism. Only in year 2000 did President Gus Dur recognize a sixth official religion, that of Confucianism), believers of each faith found peace best preserved living in distinctly separated communities. Unable to divorce themselves from the sea, the residents of Wuring elected to live just above it, in rickety huts that creaked and swayed with comforting, wavelike motion atop thin wooden stilts. These were connected by a zigzag maze of springy bamboo gangplanks made from three or four thick stems lashed together, gripped best by bare feet. Toilet was made directly into the aquamarine waters, six feet below, and washed out naturally on the receding tide.

The *Kurnia Ilahi* — the boat's name literally meant 'God Bless' — rode high at anchor and was easily distinguishable from the fully ballasted fishing vessels and outrigger canoes moored closer to shore. The ship was impaled like a florid tropical butterfly by a bright red mast. This lanced the yellow gunwale at an imprecise right angle, close to the fore. The bulk of her hull to the water line was embalmed a sober green, thereafter jaunty turquoise took over to the keel.

Flat-topped volcanoes sat brooding upon a distant horizon of mangroves. The call to midday prayer quivered from Wuring's rusting dome, the Imam's plaintive ululations distorted on shimmering waves of heat. I loaded my camera and took my first ever shot with color slide film.

Just a week before — it felt like a lifetime already — I'd been in the Vic pub, in Darwin, one of the few original buildings in that town to have survived demolition by 1974s' Typhoon Tracy. The management was celebrating its 98th anniversary: all drinks, 98 cents each. A bunch of us from the hostel, hearing of this, had rushed there to take full advantage, partying in the hot, wet, smoke-filled air stirred lazily by black paddle fans strung across the ceiling. Toby, a Swiss traveller, had convinced me to give him four rolls of black and white film in exchange for two of his Kodak Ektachrome. I'd never used professional slide film before, but he'd been in Bali and insisted I'd need chrome, "for the colors, Man." With some reluctance, and probably because I'd drunk too much, I found myself agreeing to the trade.

When Fate comes along and gives you a nudge in this way,

it usually feels uncomfortable. Change often does. But Toby was right, and my instinct to trust him proved correct. Indonesia was no country for black and white abstraction.

Gaby Fereira was Pascal's dubious local go-between—I have elected to use a pseudonym for our wily Eurasian fixer, as I am unsure about the terms and conditions of the Statute of Limitations, under Indonesian law—a squat man with shifty eyes and short attention span. His surname was inherited from his Portuguese paternal grandfather, and his business acumen handed down from earlier genetic infusions with the Dutch. I wouldn't trust him to post a letter. However, the French were forced to rely on his contacts and translation skills in negotiations with *Kurnia's* Jampea-based owner, Mr. Sauda. So, he was on the payroll, for now.

Gaby had a home and family in Maumere, but spent most of his time in Wuring, lounging in the room he rented for his young mistress, a Bugis girl, with circles of yellow chalk made from the powdered bark of the wood apple tree (*Limonia acidissima*) painted on her cheeks, providing protection from the sun. We congregated here and drank tea as Gaby hailed the sampan over from *Kurnia Ilahi* to take us out to the ship.

The Kurnia Ilahi had been constructed five years ago by the master shipbuilders of Bonerate, a Bugis island located about forty miles east-southeast of Jampea, famed for its boat-building craftsmen. A traditional *perahu* sloop, she measured seventy feet in length, weighed just over sixty tons dry, and was made entirely of wood. Her dimensions differed little from the gallant Portuguese caravels of the 15th century, whose shallow draughts and ability to tack against strong trade winds suited them perfectly to the exploration of the shallow river deltas of the African coastline. In their search for the legendary islands

filled with spices and pearls that we know today as Indonesia, such luminaries as Vasco da Gama and Christopher Columbus navigated their sturdy vessels to the very limits of the known world, and beyond. Like Columbus's ship, the *Niña*, *Kurnia Ilahi* had no engine. Nor was any single metal bolt, bracket or nail used in her frame. Her topside was decked with long planks of unbroken teak, and her sixty-foot mast still bore the smoothed branch notches of the tree trunk it had been fashioned from. An exception to tradition was the fabric of the sails, these being swathes of cheap nylon mesh, stitched together and of only slightly heavier grade and consistency than rice sacks. Pascal told me the price being asked for her was 14 million Rupiah (a not inconsiderable £5,000, at 1988 exchange rates).

The 'lifeboat' for this proud vessel was a mere sampan, a simple teak canoe, twelve feet long and barely two in width. This was capable of holding up to six adults before water started pouring over the sides. Gaby, Pascal, Franck, Fredy and I embarked in the sampan, and one of the *Kurnia's* Bugis crewmen paddled us out. I was scared to move for fear of capsizing. *Kurnia Ilahi* loomed. A rope ladder was lowered, enabling us to board.

We lazed on deck with the ship's captain, *Pak* Ambo, as official pleasantries were observed, drinking tea sweetened with condensed milk, and relishing jaunty flurries of cool air that arrived from the sea and spoke of freedom. Franck's attempt to familiarize the Bugis with his snorkeling equipment was leading to confusion—they couldn't see the use of it having been born swimming, like dolphins. Pascal and Gaby sat in furtive discussion by the tiller and were given a wide berth by all. Fredy drew the short straw. He was assigned the task of fumigating the hold. I decided to join him in the suffocating and humid bowels of the ship, our only source of illumination being a dusty beam of sunlight that angled down from the cargo hatch above. Our faces wrapped protectively in T-shirts, we sprayed industrial strength Baygon insecticide against the embedded cockroach colonies within. They dropped from the beams and lay on their backs, drowning slowly in bilge water. Half an hour of this was all I could stand, emerging with my heart beating double-time, and lungs gasping for fresh air. We dove from the deck, washing off our sweat in the tepid waters of the bay. I remained unsure whether to trust Pascal, though this could quite possibly have been a matter of cultural misunderstanding. Or maybe it was more his cozy association with Gaby I was suspicious of. He told me:

"We are planning to sail to Singapore."

Singapore was almost two thousand miles away. There was no navigational equipment on board the *Kurnia Ilahi*, not even a distress flare. I began to wonder if this voyage to France, and all the publicity he hoped to generate around it, was but an elaborate ruse to smuggle contraband across the region? I didn't fancy celebrating my second Christmas away from home banged up in Changi jail.

Worse, "We have to get there before the monsoons, in October." That left us a window of one month before the trade winds — presently blowing favorably from Flores towards Singapore — did a complete turnaround.

Later, alone in the sampan crossing back to Wuring, Gaby quizzed me on Pascal's intentions. He asked, "When are his friends really going to arrive with the rest of the money?" His suspicion was that Pascal was intentionally leaving him in the dark, and would short-change him on his commission, at the end. Then he told me, in the unspoken assumption I'd pass it on, that the original Bugis crew were becoming restless.

"They have been away from Jampea and their families for two weeks now. We cannot wait here much longer."

THE POTALA

THE POTALA PALACE thrust majestically from its rocky foundations, shrugging off soppy sentimentality and dominating the Lhasa skyline. Solid yet ephemeral, calculable yet chimerical; its zinc white buttresses and lode bearing mantles seemed to form a central pillar supporting the vast and violet firmament, providing anchorage for a religion and its people. It existed at once everywhere and yet nowhere, like the center of the Universe.

I waited for Claudia, as planned, in the *Shol*, that maze of cobbled streets, market stalls and ramshackle housing swept into a pile at the foot of the palace.

"Ah, dear idiot boy!" Claudia rushed up, smiling through her eyes, and nothing could be wrong in this world. She suggested breakfast at *The Best Place*, a budget restaurant favored by backpackers. "So, tell me, have you decided where you are heading after Lhasa? And to dispel any confusion in advance— and not wishing to influence your decision in any way—I will announce here my own intention, which is to travel to Kathmandu." With this she'd flashed a coquettish and expectant smile, leaning her chair into a dusty beam of sunlight that poured through the open window at such an angle as to inflame her golden mane and reveal she wasn't wearing a bra.

"Are all Bavarians such distractingly minimalist dressers?" I asked, surprised to hear myself change subject. My own onward travel plan was far lighter on specifics and heavier on hazard: to hitchhike east across the restricted Himalayan Plateau to Chengdu, and then sail down the Yangtze River, to Shanghai. Its formulation predated my ever having met Claudia. How could I disappoint her now, though, and tell her she took second place in the Grand Scheme of Things?

"I'll take that as a 'maybe' then," Claudia, instinctively sensing my reluctance to commit, sat upright in her chair, and started to act more business-like. "Well, let us be off then, you indecisive Brit. To the Potala." Hope and romance are both easily bruised.

We joined the eternal crowd of Tibetans shuffling in their comfy knee-length felt boots up the steep entrance ramp towards the towering white palace. A toothless old crone reached out and plucked at the hair on my arm, to check if it was real. Claudia, whose own skin was smooth and sun-browned and covered by only the slightest glaze of blonde lint, joined in, and I was overjoyed at this, our first reconciliation.

All frivolity ceased, though, as we passed the threshold and entered the secretive, flickering warren of windowless rooms; home not only to shrines and statues, but the libraries, kitchens, schoolrooms, workshops and the living quarters of hundreds of Lamas and novice monks. The thick air vibrated with their continuous humming chant— *Omm-mannni-padme-hummm* – the ringing of bells, clashing cymbals and dull thump of drums. The smell of burning oil lamps and incense was absorbed in the fetid, womb-like heat of a thousand restive candles. For some it was overpowering. Claudia stretched out her hand and we'd clung to each other like the blind, burrowing deeper and deeper into the holy foundations.

Radiating from this empyreal power-source, countless concentric rings rippled out across a troubled land. The first of these, around the base of the Potala itself, comprised a supplicant circumambulation of pilgrims, immune to commercial distraction. Some hobbled by on their knees, prostrating themselves every few feet, sliding into submission on handheld wooden blocks. Further out, less distinct yet ever-present, a flow of humble humanity navigated clockwise the market and several sacred sites around town, most notably the Jokhang Temple. "And so on, and so *Ommmm* ..." sang Claudia, "it's like ring roads around a huge metropolis."

Finally, we'd emerged, out of breath, into brilliant, unfiltered daylight on the palace rooftop. Claudia was energized, whether by proximity to prayer or just the reintroduction to fresh air. "Outside of Lhasa you see the same thing, people making circuits of the surrounding monasteries, Sera, Drepung, Gyantse, Ganden." Then she spun in a circle, arm outstretched, pointing out their rough locations. I marveled at her beauty and self-confidence. Maybe it's being so close to a living religion? These people *believed*. The more they were threatened and cajoled, the higher and further they soared from the corporeal cage.

Doubts and Diversions

Sabji and I discussed the developing situation of the *Kurnia*. We considered the possibility of joining the French as far as Jampea and then using that island as a stepping-stone to reach Sulawesi. From the main port in Sulawesi, Ujung Pandang—aka Makassar—the Indonesian government shipping line PELNI ran regular ferry services to all points of the archipelago. I had been in regular correspondence with a trio of young girls, the Said Sisters, who I'd met two months ago in Brisbane. They had been amongst the visiting groups of exchange students it had been my job to escort around the 1988 World Expo there, for a local language college. They lived in Banjarmasin on the island of Borneo, and in their last letter to me had repeated an invitation to visit. I felt a plan coming on.

It was a Tuesday, and we strolled through Maumere market, the *Pasar Selasa*—or "Tuesday Market"—which was particularly lively on its name day, each week. Here, intricately woven *ikat* sarongs, dyed in turmeric yellows and dark maroon and indigo shades obtained from mangrove bark, vied for display with trays of roasted dog flesh, bundles of live chickens, slabs of *tempeh*—the ubiquitous fermented soybean cake—wrapped in banana

leaves, and stalls selling the more prosaic daily necessities of
Rinso laundry powder, Kapal Api ground coffee, Indomie instant
noodles and Pepsodent toothpaste.

I forked out 3,500Rp. – a little over a pound – and bought a
machete, which I hung on my belt. The wild east of Indonesia,
in this respect, resembled the wild west of Tibet. I was merely
mimicking local dress etiquette, and the big knife could come in
handy for opening coconuts.

"There's Gaby," I pointed to our mediator, who was lighting
a *kretek* at a market stand. He was stooping to touch the tip of his
cigarette to a length of smoldering rope, and jumped on hearing
his name made public.

"Chris, my good friend!" he recovered quickly. His broad
grin and exhalation of smoke almost succeeded in masking the
feral calculations in his eyes, including the momentary flare of
his nostrils as he took in Sabji's long hair and flowing beard.

"Come, let us drink coffee. So, you wish to travel to Jampea?"

We straddled a long bench in a *warung* and I explained our
plan to hitch a ride on *Kurnia Ilahi* as far as the ship's home
island, and from there find alternative transport to Makassar. He
seemed to think this was a wonderful idea and we parted the
best of friends.

"I don't trust him," Sabji said as we exited the hustle of the
bazaar. These were strong words from a man ostensibly devoted
to Love, Peace and Brotherhood with Humanity.

"Neither do I," I concurred. As a rule, anyone calling you his
'good friend' upon such brief acquaintance will turn out to be
neither 'good', nor much of a 'friend'.

After breakfast, all cylinders firing on coffee and early morning
sunshine, I had a spring in my step and machete at my side. I
took a *bimo* – a cramped mini-van used as a communal taxi – and

squeezed in beside a mother breastfeeding her child for the ride to Wuring. I hailed the crew aboard *Kurnia Ilahi*, and the sampan was dispatched.

"Chris," began Pascal after I had clambered aboard, "We have been discussing it … we would like you to join us to Singapore."

I must have looked relieved. Franck smiled and offered me a mug of cringingly sweet tea, as if to seal the deal, " … but you will need to pay something." Pascal suggested the equivalent of the air ticket from Flores to Singapore, US$200. This was double the amount I'd budgeted to get there overland. I said I'd consider it, but inside I felt plunging disappointment. I'd wanted to be a part of this crew, not a paying passenger, a mere tourist.

"Oh, and I was talking to Gaby," continued Pascal. "He says anyone who arrives in Jampea will have to leave with us for Singapore. He was quite insistent." He didn't elaborate. Obviously, this ruled out the possibility of Sabji and I traveling on independently from the Bugis island to Makassar. *I think I'll call the whole thing off.*

Charly had been AWOL these last few days. His backpack had, however, remained sitting on his bed, so I knew he'd not skipped town. All was explained after breakfast, when he burst in with Stacy, a Canadian girl, in tow. They'd been off 'climbing Kelimutu', Flores's main attraction, the triple craters of the volcano being famed for their differently colored lakes. Though mountain climbing may just have been his euphemism for having sex.

He was now keen on visiting the *Kurnia Ilahi*, and professed a desire to sail to Singapore along with his countrymen. I felt a stab of jealous resentment, but accompanied him out to Wuring, all the same. Discussion onboard today was animated, and conducted almost exclusively in French. Linguistically excluded,

I wandered off with Fredy. We practiced paddling the sampan, trying to make it go in a straight line. This was harder than the Bugis made it look. A deft twist of the paddle was required to transform its flat edge from means of propulsion into a rudder. We succeeded in going around in circles, leaving the Bugis crew in hysterics.

"I am going to Bali, *mon ami*," Charly announced unexpectedly later, when we were on our way back to Maumere.

"But ... I thought you were sailing to Singapore?"

"Pascal, 'e is a good man. You need not worry about eem. But I cannot stand zis type, always being ze boss. I 'ave to go my own way, you know that." He then revealed the real reason behind Gaby's caveat about everyone having to sail on to Singapore. "Eet is not you, *mon ami*. Eet is Sabji. Gaby says ze Bugis don't like 'im. Zey are all Muslim and 'ee looks like Jesus. And on Jampea only women 'ave long 'air."

That evening, in return for a pack of *kreteks*, I was able to extract from Gaby the full story of why the Bugis had taken such offence to Sabji's appearance.

"Traditional Bugis," he muttered through a lazily exhaled stream of smoke, "believe there are five genders, and that all five must exist in harmony. Okay?" He paused, and I nodded that I was on track with him, so far. "These are male and female — 'oroane' and 'makkunrai'. Then you have 'calabai', you know, a false woman," he picked at his teeth.

"What we call a gay male?"

"Yes, yes. That will be it. These calabai, they take on the roles of the female and are very good to organize weddings."

"That's three genders already. What comes next?" I asked Gaby, intrigued by the unexpected level of sexual tolerance being shown by, what until now, I'd thought was a rather conservative

46

society.

"Well, now it starts to get interesting," replied Gaby, warming to the topic. "Next you get the 'calalai'. These are the females who dress and act like men." These would come closest to the western concept of lesbians. The most unique of all, however, were the fifth gender, known as the 'bissu'.

"Bissu are fearsome and longhaired. They have no sex gender and are said to hold supernatural powers!" Gaby paused to take a sip from his coffee. I ordered us another round.

"Yes, the bissu — I saw one, once — they are frowned upon by orthodox Islamic society but are tolerated in Bugis lands where they are praised for their fortune-telling abilities and black magic."

So, it appeared our Bugis crewmen had mistaken the mild-mannered hippie, Sabji, not as a re-embodiment of Jesus Christ but, instead, as a far more threatening and disruptive western version of one of their own transgender witch doctors. No wonder they had been nervous about transporting him to their island!

I felt a wave of pity for poor Sabji. But the icing on the cake was applied later, when I caught up with Charly, and he remembered:

"Oh, and Pascal says don't worry about ze money, just pay for your share of supplies." He leaned close, "Zey need you. Zey are only six men, and eet takes that many just to raise ze sail. So, you are in luck *mon brave*, you will 'ave to steer."

That night, back at the *Bogor Hotel*, Sabji greeted me, all apologetic.

"Sorry Chris, I'm bailing, man. This Canadian chick says there's a PELNI ship from Ende next week, it's cheap and has life vests." And, just like that, I was released from the onerous duty of informing him that his choice of hairstyle was offensive to the superstitious Bugis of Jampea.

Somewhat at random, I flipped to a passage in *The Handbook of Chinese Horoscopes*, I found lying around the hotel lobby.

"I am the kaleidoscope of the mind.
I impart light, color and perpetual motion.
I think, I see, I am moved by electric fluidity.
Constant only in my inconstancy,
I am shackled by mundane holds,
Unchecked by sturdy, binding goals.
I run unimpeded through virgin paths.
My spirit unconquered –
My soul forever free.
I am the Horse."

It is not only significant people we come across by chance, but books as well. I am a Horse. And this was me. Or at least the version of me I'd like to be.

That morning, Pascal, Franck and Fredy moved from the ship to join me in town at the *Bogor Hotel*, there being so much left to organize in Maumere before setting sail. They were out now, at the airstrip, acquiring an accurate time reading, and had taken my watch with them. All our timepieces needed to be synchronized, keeping one on GMT. This was essential for navigational purposes, apparently. Pascal had brought an impressive sextant with him from France, and would be taking readings, each day at noon. He himself had decided to wait in Maumere for the rest of the crew – Xavier, Gilles and Bruno – to arrive from France. The costly long-distance telephone call he'd made to Paris the night before had shed no light on the whereabouts of this tardy trio. Since the Bugis were restive to the point of rebellion, Franck, Fredy and myself elected to go ahead and sail on *Kurnia* to Jampea, taking along Gaby for emergency translations. Gaby was less than happy about this. He would have preferred to stay close to Pascal, and the money.

Fredy and I were tasked with buying supplies. Before entering the market, I popped into the bank to exchange a traveler's check, as Franck warned there would be no banks on Jampea. The teller took his own sweet time. He seemed primarily interested in practicing his English and in finding out how much Pascal was being overcharged for the *Kurnia Ilahi*. To my bafflement, it seemed the whole of bloody Maumere knew about our voyage; a condition Franck was later able to clear-up.

It had happened some ten days before Charly and I had arrived in Maumere (and how I rued not having been witness to the scene):

"Pascal and Fredy were out, busy organizing some shit at the market or somewhere, so Pascal he told me, 'go to the bank and exchange all the money we have' — this is maybe half the cost of the boat — 20 or 30,000 francs in traveler's checks. A shit load of francs," he blew out a stream of smoke, lost in the memory. We were back on board *Kurnia* at the time, Franck resting against the outer cabin wall, picking at loose flakes of tobacco from a hand-rolled cigarette that had lodged between his teeth. He continued, "in exchange for an even shittier, much larger, load of rupiah. The transaction was so huge they had to close the bank; all the tellers were needed to count out our notes. Later I came out with these two huge black sacks full of rupiah, dragging them down the steps. They were really heavy." Being Indonesia, word had spread, and many people had gathered to watch the spectacle.

"Funny, I had no single thought of being robbed of all this money. I just jumped into a *bimo* and back to *Kurnia*."

49

Back to the present day, and we still had to provision for a dozen souls on board for the anticipated two-to-three-day hop to Jampea island. Therefore, we hired a man with a handcart who followed us as we scurried around the bazaar. He transported our growing pile of potatoes, bananas, instant noodles, coffee, condensed milk, dried fish, chili sauce, paraffin cooking fuel, and toilet paper (another luxury that would be unavailable on Jampea), and guarded against casual pilferage. He tut-tutted at how much each stallholder was ripping us off, but the traders just laughed, complicit in the game. The total came to about £15. Feeling generous, I threw in two cartons of *kreteks* for the crew, the Gudang Garam brand, which was higher quality than the foul sticks they usually smoked.

At 4:15 p.m. I bid Charly *adieu*. It seemed unlikely we'd be bump into each other again for a long time since, after Australia, he planned to head to South America. So I judged it of historical importance to note the precise time in my diary. Pascal, Franck, Fredy and I commandeered a *bimo* to transfer all our new supplies to Wuring. It took us three trips in the sampan to manhandle everything on board. While I was waiting for the sampan to return, Gaby's girlfriend idly brushed the hair on my arm, and then ran off with my hat, hiding it in her bedroom. One of the Bugis rubbed his fingers and thumb together, indicating I could follow her in there, for a price. The girl shook her hand 'no' at his implication, pouting theatrically. Both ended up laughing, and I joined in. Nothing in Indonesia appeared so serious it couldn't be resolved with a smile.

We were set to depart at sunset. Once aboard *Kurnia*, Pascal came over to me.

"Chris, I want you to document the trip with your camera," he said. "Later on, when it gets here, you help Franck with the video, yes? Cover everything, repairs, daily life, no detail is unimportant." It was a responsibility I was happy to shoulder. Like a proud shopkeeper, he took a final stock check around the ship before a crewman paddled him ashore. Ignoring the smaller vessel's inherent instability, he stood fully upright in the sampan, waving goodbye as it receded, a wobbly Washington crossing an equatorial Delaware. Last to board was Gaby. "You forgot your hat," he said, handing over the offending item, his eyes glowing like cigarette tips.

Maneuvering out of Wuring bay with no engine and little wind taxed even our crew of experienced Bugis seamen. The *Kurnia Ilahi* possessed three anchors. Whilst five men were required to weigh the heaviest of these, several others paddled out in the sampan to drop off the two smaller anchors at the limit of their ropes. From the main deck, we pulled on these ropes, inching the vessel forward and around, a technique known by its deceptive nautical term as 'warping' — tediously slow, and far from the 'warp speed' used by Captain Kirk in *Star Trek*.

A ghost of a breeze fluttered through the jib, then the triangular sail half filled. Slowly, imperceptibly, we began to move. The rigging tensed and cracked as the giant ship awakened from her slumber. After a few minutes we passed the outer reef. Six of us hauled up the mainsail as the mast creaked in protest. Water started rushing past the bow, and the deck tilted a few degrees off the horizontal.

We were sailing!

NOTES ON THE WIND

ON A DIFFERENT ocean, in an older world — one in which frozen waves of ice-clad Tibetan peaks struggle to nourish woven tufts of sage like the algae-covered backs of a circling pod of leviathans — I remember the wind. Not this humid, taunting, equatorial torpor, but an irresistible, scudding howl released from the very top of the world, urgent to deliver news of distant glinting *gompas*; one carrying on its breath the plaintive desires committed to countless ragged prayer flags. A furious messenger, emboldening whorls of dust to rise in the courtyards of numerous, vine-draped caravansary; one that forces heads to bow and hat brims be clutched at.

And yet it is the same wind. The same wind that, connected by invisible stratospheric currents and governed by immutable meteorological laws, caresses and tempts the surface of the Java Sea into pale white crests, tugs wistfully at our sails, and teases wooden pulley blocks to slap hollowly against the mast: a wind that acts in distant and involuntary obeisance to the tempestuous whims of a frigid Himalayan counterpart. It is a wind that, this month, blows with all confidence towards the northwest, and the next will turn on its heels and shamelessly blow to the southeast.

Can we accuse the wind of being fickle? Does it not know where it is going, or simply fail to care? 'North', 'south', 'east', 'west', what are these but human concepts of creation and division, anyway?

Back then, seated high in the back of a *Jeifang* truck, I'd skimmed across a landscape as dry and empty as the moon, the wind in my face, a leaf carried on a steely breeze: I'd never been so free, so far removed from responsibility.

I knew I *belonged* to this world of transit. Like a nomad, my home was the opportunity for adventure offered between the absolutes of departure and arrival. Alienation, prejudice: these conditions, I'd thought, only arise once you become attached to a place or person. And I'd resolved to move continually forward, renouncing any claim to colony or companion.

The wind is like that nomad, and rarely a threat. Placing no strain on patience or resource, it moves on tomorrow, unlikely to pass this way again. Momentarily it invigorates those huddled around the campfire with distant tales and reminders of a freedom they once dreamt of for themselves.

The wind is restless. Tireless it pursues its destiny, discarding as it goes memories of loss and regret, sadness and elation. And from somewhere, carried far away from a lush summer meadow in the middle of a Tibetan stream, the scent of honey, wildflowers and wood smoke reaches me across the frothing peaks of this unpredictable and murky sea, wishing to speak to me of love.

I am here, Claudia; you've found me. Can I trust this wind to lead me to you?

GABY CONFESSES

WE ENDURED A listless first day at sea. Since setting out from Maumere, the only thing we'd achieved was to drift past its main offshore feature, Palu island ... slowly. I lost all my games of chess with Franck. Mimicking the lethargy of the wind, and with no emergencies to challenge them, the crew dozed on the open deck, mummified in their sarongs; and Franck, Fredy, Gaby and I rested inside the three-foot high, windowless cabin. Directly below us, bilge water sloshed about in the hull, it's rhythm oddly reassuring. At night, a lone crewman hung on the tiller. I asked him how he knew where he was going with no compass to guide him, and he pointed to a *bintang*, a star. *This one*, he said, is *Jampea*. Another was for Kupang, Makassar, Surabaya. And in the daytime, when there were no stars? *I just hold her in a straight line*, he gestured, *she knows her own way home*.

The crew prepared all our meals. These comprised bananas with sweet cakes and condensed milk tea, for breakfast; and rice with dried fish and noodles the rest of the time. I noticed that they were still smoking their same old hand-rolled cigarettes, saving the Gudang Garams to trade with on Jampea. The Bugis were more professional and serious at sea. They had a reputation to uphold. But they couldn't disguise their curiosity, following us into the cabin each time we retreated from the sun, eager to see what wonders we would pull forth from our backpacks next. Each member of the crew *had* to try on the headphones of Franck's Walkman, each astounded – in turn – by the miraculous sound created. And what was the correct protocol surrounding the distribution of medicines? Achmed, for example, complained of a pain in his back. He was *so* insistent I called in 'Doctor Fredy' for a consultation. He advised, "Give him an aspirin, or something."

I made a show of carefully opening the tin foil of a strip of bitter nivaquine malaria pills, and then compelled Achmed to crush one in his mouth before swallowing. He winced before springing to life, reborn by my marvel pill. Soon they were all queuing with a litany of complaints, most common of which being an inadequacy of the male member.

At 7 p.m. the helmsman started whistling a monotonous tune to call up the wind. His prayers were answered; frail vespers soon arrived, evaporating the sweat from our bodies in their cool ascending spiral. We manhandled the boom starboard across the roof of the cabin, forcing the ship to tack and make best use of these feint gusts; soon the breeze stiffened, the mainsail snapped and billowed. Nature took over.

The creaking of the boat awakened me at dawn, sunlight streaming in through the roof hatch. We were drifting languidly again, being bullied by the waves, and had gained only about ten miles in the night. I made sure to take a full quarter of an hour to brush my teeth; it would be a long day, and there was nothing much else to do in it. My choice of outfit was straightforward enough: I had decided to wear only shorts – no shoes, shirt or even underwear – all the while at sea. My body, like every surface on the *Kurnia Ilahi*, was sticky with salt spray. This sea mist was creating havoc, misting up my camera's lens filter, but I couldn't risk wiping it and scratching its surface.

Gaby stooped to enter the cabin, Franck and I absently completing what must have been our hundredth game of blackjack. He pored over my map of Southeast Asia, frustrated by our lack of progress; he was, he said, used to boats with engines.

"I have worked all over Indonesia, from Java to Irian Jaya (the Indonesian, western half of the island of New Guinea, known today as West Papua) to Kalimantan ... the Taiwanese and Korean ships take the logs and pay very well for my services." He wanted to remind us of his worth. "Here," he jabbed my map at a point south of Banjarmasin where the massive Barito River lets into the Java Sea, "you will know when you get this far, the water becomes yellow with mud washed out, at least this far." He casually scored a line some hundred kilometers distant from the shore with his thumbnail. Gaby, like many Indonesians, opted to grow his fingernails long, signaling his degree of separation from demeaning physical labor. "I have money. I have friends everywhere. I know everything that goes on." It sounded more threat than boast, and he stared at me, specifically, whilst delivering it. And then he paused and emitted an involuntary gasp, as though stunned by a sudden view hacked-out along some overgrown mental pathway. From nowhere, he whipped out a flashing stiletto blade and stabbed it right into the island of Buru.

"And here ... I killed a man."

It had happened some years ago. Gaby, in a hurry to depart Buru (the third largest of the Maluku islands, and President Suharto's tropical gulag for around 12,000 political prisoners) had engaged a rickshaw to transport him to his ship. "The driver started to take me to a bad area, where all the gangsters live. If

I wait too long, I know it is too late, there will be too many of these villains waiting, so I start yelling and he stops the rickshaw, pulling out a long machete. I hit him in the face first, and he goes down bleeding. Luckily, we are on a bridge, so I pick him up by the belt and throw him over the edge. Hah! And then I ride his rickshaw and catch my ship."

Seven-twenty in the morning, Greenwich Mean Time – 3:20 p.m., local time. Though the only references you can be sure of are sunrise, sunset and the scalding deck of noon. Grey clouds brought rain, a chance for us to cleanse the decks, and a strong gusting wind. The jib billowed and *Kurnia Ilahi*, until now an old nag, resignedly ambling along, transformed into a thoroughbred. The Bugis sprang into action tightening ropes, and the ship, no longer slave to their deeper persuasions, started scudding over the waves, instead. The island of Bonerate became visible ahead on the starboard horizon.

At sunset I inched out to the very tip of the prow, clinging to *Kurnia Ilahi's* forward jib stay. I dangled my feet either side of the main spar and sat suspended and gliding ten feet above the dark waves. And then the ship plunged, taking my breath away. The prow dove into the void, heading for the pit of the ocean before, juddering, the ship began to recover. My bare soles skated the sea's surface, leaving a sparkling trail of electric green plankton as we surfed the upward swell. I clung to the neck of this flighty wooden dolphin – alone in the universe, surrounded by blackness – deprived of any sense of bearing or gravity. Only the breeze, still warmed by the memory of the sun, alerted me to place in time, hitting my face from the unseen future, on its way to a forgotten past.

PART
2

JAMPEA ISLAND PARADISE
Jampea Island
Monday, 5th September 1988

CAPTAIN OF THE *Kurnia Ilahi*, *Pak* Ambo, was a tubby, mild-mannered man. He had inherited his position, along with his wife, a daughter of the ship's owner *Pak* Sauda. With delicate fingers and receding hairline he appeared more bookkeeper than buccaneer. He wore the uncomfortable costume assigned him by Fate and family genially enough, and had kept a low profile during the voyage. This morning, though, we awoke to a general scramble on deck, Ambo directing operations, the conductor of an unruly orchestra. Jampea had crept up during the night, sunrise now revealing the deep folds in her verdant dress. The crew prepared to drop anchor in the horseshoe bay of their homeport. Ambo's eldest son Achmed readied the sampan, scooping out bilge water with a tin plate.

Palm trees, thatched huts, the glint of sun on a tin minaret: the basic ingredients of settlement throughout the Java Sea. The recipe here was augmented by a floating side dish of *perahu* — similar in design to the *Kurnia Ilahi*, though none as colorful — rickety shrimp platforms, and a fleet of canoes, heading our way in greeting.

We made landfall next to *Pak* Sauda's toilet, a knee-high box raised on poles three feet above the water, accessed by a coconut wood plank: a vantage point from which to see, and be seen (indeed, so curious as to our biological diversity from theirs became some of the villagers, that I was surrounded on this shoreline perch after the evening meal by spectators eager to see if my poo was white, like my skin).

We washed our feet with water from pails drawn from a well in the ship-owner's courtyard as scrawny chickens darted about underfoot, and a gallery of women and children played peek-a-boo from behind lacy curtains, above. Fredy presented *Pak* Sauda with a carton of *kreteks*, a few packs of which were opened, the individual sticks fanned out in teacups and offered around. Gaby seemed unusually taciturn, removed from his Maumere powerbase, wary of how to explain Pascal's absence. When the ritual pleasantries of sweet tea and small talk reached a natural lull, he urged Franck, Fredy and I to follow him outside.

"Come. You have to report with your passports to the police."

The law on Jampea was enshrined in the person of *Pak* Hussein (*Bapak*, mostly shortened to *Pak*, being a universal honorific, similar to 'Sir' or 'Mr.'). School was out and a small army of tiny children, dressed in uniform red and white, followed us to the policeman's door. We removed our shoes and were ushered into the cool shade by Hussein's wife, a handsome woman, with the bearing of a schoolmistress. She insisted the protocol of tea and biscuits be observed (basking in our praise of her culinary proficiency, she said she'd bake a new batch just for us, tomorrow) before explaining her husband was presently out.

My eyes swept the room. His machete, twin gun holsters, a whistle, tape measure and jacket hung on the back of the door, along with the obligatory portraits of a grinning President Suharto, and his gaunt VP, Sudharmono. There was a framed picture of Hussein's parents, too. An adjoining wall was covered in photos; one showing the black box in Mecca, replete with streaming pilgrims, another, his certificate of police training. Several posters featured scantily clad Asian girls handling Kalashnikovs, one of them astride a high-powered Japanese motorcycle. And there were two posters featuring Sylvester Stallone as *Rambo*.

A deep snore reverberated from within, beyond the curtains of the rear room. Diplomatically, we said we'd return with our documents, later, after *Pak* Hussein 'came back'. On the way out, my attention was caught by two remarkably detailed model boats; there was a similar, larger version, in *Pak* Sauda's house.

"*Bapak* Ambo makes them," the policeman's wife informed us with evident pride. We all need one, an artistic outlet. Ambo's, it would seem, was rampant, and his models were really rather good.

Later, *Pak* Hussein paid us a visit at Ambo's house, where Franck, Fredy and I had been consigned to sleep. Off duty and out of uniform, he carried a service revolver in the waistband of his sarong. He studied my passport carefully, upside down, and Franck pointed out, with due deference, the Indonesian visa, this, presumably, being among the first he had encountered. With formalities concluded, Hussein was all smiles. He insisted on accompanying us on a stroll along Jampea's sandy main alley. The path was rutted, wide and completely empty — there being no motor vehicles on Jampea — and it paralleled the beach. Soon this majestic boulevard deteriorated into a single file grass track, shaded by towering coconut palms.

All was silent, bar the rippling clack of their fronds disturbed by the wind high above; the distant pulse of crashing waves; and the faint, intermittent mechanical buzz of chainsaws, from the interior. Saltwater ponds marked the end of the settlement.

Hussein took out his pistol and shot randomly at all the fish in the water. They survived today's fusillade. On the way back we were intercepted by Ambo's youngest son, Ahmod, out of breath from running to find us. He panted: *Pascal and the others have just come ashore!* Their delay was soon explained: the flight from Paris had transited through Bangkok, and the notorious diversions of Patpong Road, with its litany of seedy girlie bars.

Kicking up a trail of dust, we rushed back in the direction of *Pak* Sauda's spacious compound, where a crowd of islanders had gathered to examine the new arrivals. I was just as curious as they to see what my new shipmates looked like.

Now, in matters of personality, I trust my gut, and my gut told me I could trust the personality of Gilles-Marie. After all, *his* gut was sizeable. 'Big Gilles', as the rest gently chided him, was a man obviously fond of consumption. Gregarious by nature, his command of English was better than all but Fredy's, as though unwilling to allow any pesky foreign word restrict his access to pleasure. In stark contrast to Gilles, who even at this early stage I could see wore his emotions both up and down his sleeve, Bruno was introspective, brooding and gangly. He either knew no English or chose not to use it. This air of distant loftiness suited him well. Possessed of only a few stock phrases of French myself, I hoped I appeared to him similarly exotic. A sizeable Evreux clique existed, with Gilles, Pascal, Franck and Bruno all hailing from that understated town in the flatlands of Normandy. And then there was Xavier. He and Pascal had already crossed the Sahara together, on several occasions, by both motorcycle and car, and were no strangers either to each other, or to risk. Xavier was groomed, sophisticated, adult, and worked for Remy Martin, in Cognac. I make no claim to being an expert on French cinema, but there were suggestions in his looks and gestures of a young Alain Delon in *Les Aventuriers*.

THE PRICE OF A BRIDE

I HAD SET my alarm for 5 a.m., but the damned cockerels woke me first. A few minutes later, their crowing merged with the call of the mosque, and I really *couldn't* stay in bed any longer.

Fortunately, having always been a morning person, it gave me a buzz to be up before most of the rest of the world. I relished that sense of belonging to a select group. The malignant creatures of the night, exhausted of their evil urges, were all in bed now, and it was safe for the world to start afresh. There was something optimistic about the delicacy of the light at this time, too, helping bring to life colors purer and more fleeting than those of the industrial afternoon and populist sunset.

Fredy and I headed out to film sunrise on the waterfront, where silhouetted boats lay beached like whales on the low tide. The locals were getting used to seeing us around now. One man bounded up a coconut tree aided by ropes tied around his ankles. He lopped off a few *kelapa muda*, the fresh young fruits: their skins were thick and they had only a thin edible flesh, but there was over a pint of juice contained in each. Climbing back down from the dizzying tree, he carved a V-shaped drinking hole in two of these, using a few deft swipes of his machete, and handed Fredy and I one each.

The video camera was surprisingly simple to use. We were dragged in to record one couple—rare among Jampeans in having left the island—and they, after an acceptable display of modest resistance, yielded to public demand and dressed-up in the magnificent costumes they'd worn on their Haj to Saudi Arabia.

"The Bugis girls are very pretty and they are used to their men being away for much of the time." Gaby had crept right up beside me. He could just as easily have thrust his switchblade between my ribs, into my heart.

"You can pay for a wife here, you know ..." he continued, casually.

"For how much?" asked Fredy, as though considering buying one to release in the wild.

"Usually 1.5 million Rupiah, some of the ugly ones you can get for a million. They all know their bride price and will be happy to tell you." Once again, I was priced out of the market. "Yes, and if a man does not pay this dowry but makes love to a Bugis girl anyway, then it means death to the girl, her unborn child and the man ... if he is fool enough to ever step foot on these islands again."

I held Gaby's gaze, hoping he'd see I was innocent of any charge. It was Gaby, surprisingly, who changed subject.

"I hear," he said, "that one of Sauda's daughters has her eye on Pascal. Her husband disappeared a few years ago. She has a child, but she is not painful to look at." Describing any daughter of *Pak* Sauda as being the one 'with child' didn't much narrow the field. Sauda had many daughters, and even the youngest of these—who looked to me no more than fourteen—had two kids already. I assured him I'd pass the information on to Pascal. Possibly Gaby intended it as a peace offering. Franck informed

me later that Pascal would pay Gaby a bonus if he could persuade
the wily ship owner to agree to sell *Kurnia Ilahi* for 11 million Rp.,
not the 13.5 million negotiations had been stalled at these last
two days.

"Though I suspect Gaby has had a better offer from Sauda,"
Franck speculated. All this intrigue was infectious. Wherever
we wandered people invited us to their verandas, plied us with
tea and cakes and pumped us for the latest update on The Deal.
So far, every household we had entered, without exception, had
had one of Ambo's intricate model boats on display, their size
and elaborateness of design reflecting the island's strict order of
social hierarchy.

I faced a dilemma. To proceed directly to Singapore on *Kurnia
Ilahi*, without seeing anything of Indonesia, seemed abrupt,
wasteful. Not to mention, hazardous. Gaby had mentioned a
local fisherman, *Pak* Diep, who was apparently willing to take
me on his boat to Selayar, from which island a regular ferry
operated to the Sulawesi mainland. But I was wary of Gaby's
intentions, even if his unsubstantiated vendetta was nothing
more than the product of my own growing paranoia. Pascal and
Gaby were more alike than their egos would ever admit: a dark,
disruptive streak lurked in both their souls. At least death on the
Kurnia would befall us communally, by misadventure. I found
this preferable, in the end, to the thought of being knifed and
dumped as shark-bait, alone, in the Sulawesi shallows.

Fredy, Bruno and I shared no direct financial investment in
the *Kurnia Ilahi* enterprise. As such, we were excluded from the
increasingly voluble negotiations taking place in *Pak* Sauda's
shadowy, spacious living room. Since we could offer only our
sweat, toil and youthful enthusiasm to the proceedings, we
instead assisted the Bugis crew in removing *Kurnia's* existing
ballast of crumbling coral and rock—which had a tendency to

roll around a bit too much in rough seas. This we replaced with twenty-seven rice sacks, each filled with 50kgs of sand, and requiring a dozen trips back and forth in the sampan to complete.

Despite our sterling efforts the ship still swayed light and free atop the translucent waters of the bay, as though she'd float into the clouds if not tethered to the ocean floor by her anchor chain.

Dog Bites and Destiny

I WAS WANDERING through the market scattered alongside Jokhang Temple, preoccupied, selecting some small, silk embroidered panels featuring the Buddha that would make nice gifts to post home, when a mangy dog, half wolf, lunged at me from out of the shadows. Luckily, I caught the movement out the corner of my eye and was able to turn and avoid the worst of its bite. Stallholders rushed in *en masse*, throwing pebbles and scaring the hound away. Blood began to ooze through my sock, and made me feel faint. I limped back to the *Yak Guesthouse* to clean and sterilize the wound with iodine, apply some Savlon, and tie it all up in a bandage (my first aid kit finally coming in handy). Claudia, who had been somewhat distant since our afternoon beside the river, rallied to my side.

"Lucky you didn't get bitten in Afghanistan. They have the highest rate of rabies in the world there." Very helpful. But I was happy to have her back again, and implicitly trusted in her diagnosis:

"You have between one to three months for the neurological symptoms to show…"

I interrupted her, "So, plenty of time to get to a hospital in

Chengdu, then?" I said, relieved.

"*Nein*," in her mother tongue, frustrated by my sunny optimism, "by then it is too late. When you start to experience the symptoms, you have only a few days before certain death."

"What should I do, then?" I was suddenly deflated.

"You require a series of vaccine jabs over the course of two weeks."

"Two *weeks*? I can't stay here that long!"

"Or else you could die. Two weeks in Lhasa doesn't seem too long compared to eternity dead." Only there turned out to be no rabies vaccine available at the main Lhasa clinic, or anywhere else in town.

A circuit of the market failed to track down the offending hound, to see how crazed it looked, and foaming of mouth. Giving up, we decided the next best option would be to consume far too many bottles of Lhasa Beer at *The Best Place*. It ended up becoming a raucous send-off, especially after some other travelers from our guesthouse spotted us and joined in. *I may die before reaching Chengdu. Cheers!* The thought left me oddly light-headed. Acting against her own immediate self-interest and desire, Claudia relented. She handed over to me a tiny map, torn from the pages of her Chinese atlas. This revealed, across six inches of paper, the road from Lhasa to Chengdu, with major settlements along the way written in miniature Chinese characters. Two thousand kilometers of torturous, airless terrain, and multiple, five-thousand-meter-high passes.

"I know it is pointless to try to persuade you to change your mind, so at least take this and try not to get lost," she said.

Claudia's bicycle was parked outside. I rode us unsteadily home on it, she perched primly, sideways on the rack, arms hugging my waist, her head rested on my back, both of us bobbing up and down with the motion of the pedals.

The sky turned a premature dark prune color; the temperature plummeted, and large dollops of rain began to explode on the dusty cobbled streets. I doubled my efforts to get us back to the *Yak*, tossing the bike into the courtyard, Claudia racing ahead, fighting to hold the door open against a violent gust, "Hurry, Chris!"

I barely made it inside before the sandstorm hit. And there we stood in the sudden stillness of the corridor breathing hard, the door rattling. I looked down into her reddened eyes, her pupils glinting and magnified with tears:

"Come with me, Chris. We can go to Nepal. They have the rabies vaccine there. We can be together ..."

"There's nothing I'd like more, Claudia ... but," I blustered and faded. *But what?* I didn't even know, myself. Was I really willing to throw away, so casually, the sure offer of companionship and the road to Kathmandu, the certain cure for rabies ... the possibility of sex?

Why do you always make life so difficult for yourself? I heard my mother sigh, in mock exasperation. And then I understood what deep down I had always known: that true adventure can only be had by stepping into the unknown, alone. It is an act of faith. And I'd been preparing myself for this departure, without realizing it, through all those hours as a teenager poring over intricately inscribed maps on the living room floor; imagining the scenery crossed by that thin red line, clinging to the contours of the Himalayas, and heading — always — to the East.

Now was no time for hesitation. Destiny demands resolve. In reward it lures us to places we can only dream of, and then hands us responsibility over life and death. I swallowed the lump rising in my throat and clung tighter to Claudia, the tempest shrieking and moaning in protest at its exclusion from our tryst.

"Maybe it's best this way."

"Idiot boy," she sighed, and then blessed my journey with a deep and lingering kiss.

I'll always remember this chapter of ours on the top of the world, squeezed between the bookends of two sandstorms.

A Deal is Struck

A RIOT WAS erupting on the village football ground, 'Rambo' Hussein furiously blasting on his whistle. Dodging about in midfield trying to control an unruly scrum of two dozen boys, he played both referee and star striker in the strongest team. Fredy and I were inducted into the side opposite him in an attempt to level a rather one-sided match. We were not much help — our side went down 7–2 — but not before Fredy struck a blow for justice, bringing Hussein down with a sliding tackle of some beauty. The crowd and players erupted in cheers: they would never have dared challenge the policeman themselves.

Leaving our shoes to be nibbled at by his goats, we ascended the smoothed wooden staircase to *Pak* Sauda's residence. Inside, Pascal, Franck, Xavier and Gilles were shouting at each other, the Bugis contingent looking on in embarrassed confusion. Gaby, glad of our interruption, used the opportunity to slink away. A moment of calm descended. Pascal, red in the face, lit a cigarette. Women bustled in bearing trays of tea and cakes, mindful to keep their heads lower than those of the assembled men, as Bugis custom dictated.

The son of a Bern butcher, Fredy had been granted rare

access to the mysterious female bastion of the kitchen. It was to here, amid the steaming kettles and bubbling pots of broth and severed fish heads, that we retreated during this momentary truce around the high table. Fredy squatted down, intent on continuing his lesson from Sauda's wife about some specific culinary preparations for our upcoming voyage.

"These guys are pirates," Fredy whispered, confirming my deepest fears about the Bugis, and Gaby in particular. "They want to sail off as soon as possible, and screw the consequences."

"Oh... you mean Pascal?" I stuttered.

"All of the French," he explained, simultaneously engaging with Sauda's womenfolk, who were showing him how to stuff a sticky rice dessert with brown sugar. "I think Sauda will agree to their offer, just to get us all out of his house and off his island. He's a pretty reasonable sort, fortunately."

Possibly this had been the French bargaining strategy all along. By nightfall, to the hissing witness of hurricane lamps, a deal was struck, 11 million Rp. And *Pak* Sauda got to keep his outboard motor, as a concession. We never *could* fix that to the sampan without it sinking, anyway. Pascal smiled for the first time in days.

At 10 p.m., the diesel generator supplying our end of the village spluttered and died. There was no alternate source of electricity on the island, other than that stored in the car batteries used on some of the fishing vessels. Fredy and I accompanied Ambo back to his house, padding along sandy, moonlit tracks. It was too dark to make out the expression on the captain's face. It had been a long day, and those cockerels would be up again in no time at all.

HAJI BAJU

HAJI BAJU WASN'T really a Haji at all; he could never afford the trip to Mecca. Besides, leaving the island would mean traveling on the sea, and that was something he'd given up doing a long time ago. Still, the local kids honored him with the pilgrims' title, skipping and dancing and calling his name *A-jee-ba-joo* in singsong, leading us out to where the fishponds flooded over at high tide, trapping flounders behind his dykes as the waters receded.

He was out wading, waist-deep in one of his ponds when we first saw him. Spotting us, his face opened to reveal a piano key smile, and he reached out with big muddy hands and long boney fingers: ideal for grabbing and keeping hold of wriggling fishes, for filleting and beheading. The Gollum of the salt estuary. Haji Baju collected a new net and invited Fredy and I to join him in the pool.

We took off our shoes, gasping as our thighs sank in the boiling, gooey sludge. The fisherman had already laid out his circular net. Instantly fish began jumping to the surface, thrashing, becoming entangled in its mesh. In just three minutes, Haji Baju had caught fourteen beautiful eight-ounce fishes,

offering them to us for dinner. The Bugis language has no phrase for "Thank you", so we passed on our gratitude in the common Indonesian tongue: "*Terimakasih!*"

His nickname, *Baju*, or 'shirt' was gained at sea. The young Daeng — as he was known in childhood — had been swept off the deck of a *pinisi* (the traditional Bugis schooner; a twin-masted wooden sailing ship, often reaching 100-feet in length) and carried away in the palm of a giant wave. Given up for dead by his crewmates, he had followed a bright orange shirt flapping on the stern deck of the vanishing ship.

The Bugis are well known for their dead-reckoning skills, blessed from birth by some multi-dimensional, gyroscopic ability that allows them to calculate — from incremental changes in the shape of a wave, hue of the water, scent of the spray, direction of the wind and position of the stars — precisely where they are and in which direction they need to keep going. Don't expect an answer as to how they reach this conclusion; they just *know*. Daeng, with steely determination, fixed his gaze upon this faintest of orange stars, calculated the course his instincts told him to be correct, and doggedly began to swim. He washed up the next day, upon the very rocks his ship had been smashed, all hands lost. He vowed never to sail again, opting instead to catch his fish on land.

Multiple Exposures

FREED FROM SMOKY negotiations, Franck was back in charge of the video camera, and we continued our documentary of the sleepy daily drama of Jampea. I was intrigued to see how my own photographs would turn out. The sun, this close to the equator, was unforgiving. It climbed rapidly and gazed down with withering eye. Sandy beaches became blinding snowfields that easily fooled my camera's light meter. Like Haji Baju, I learned to outsource my essential readings to multiple sources: from the shaded grove of bamboo to the constant blue of the sky, and the gleaming metal roof of the primary school. My senses darted, calculating all extremes and shades of light, paring them down to a single, organic average — distilling the very waves of mystic nature down into a definitive F-stop on my aperture ring, and a fraction of a second for my shutter speed.

Word had spread that we were putting on a show tonight. The local administrative building, one of the few concrete structures on the island, just happened to house Jampeas' only color television set. And Xavier had worked out how to plug our video recorder into it.

We arrived early in the evening, pushing past excitable,

smoking villagers and their spicy forest fire of crackling *kreteks*. The air was thick with the fragrance of sweet tobacco and burnt clove as the zesty buds embedded in each cigarette sparked and popped when consumed by fire, giving the sticks their onomatopoeic name.

Inside Pascal, as usual, was in command and getting frustrated:

"Tournez-la et pointez-la par la fenêtre, c'est la seule façon!" he shouted to Xavier who began to manhandle the TV set, pointing it out the window and introducing to Jampea, by this simple maneuver, the concept of open-air cinema. Ambo and his sons beat back the inquisitive crowd, many of whom now scrambled out to join the congregation in the courtyard.

Outside, three hundred people—more arriving every minute—jostled for position in front of the small screen. Some teetered on chairs at the back, others clung to the crow's nest of an overhanging coconut tree, and a table became a teeming poop deck offering a view across the surging sea of heads. *Pak* Sauda attempted a few words of polite introduction, Pascal by his side, but was drowned out in cheers and expectant chatter.

A momentary silence fell as the TV sparked into life, swallowed up in the tempest of hooting and good-natured jeering that erupted as soon as people recognized themselves and their friends on the flickering screen. Halfway through the film's second twenty-minute run, the crowd increasingly raucous now they were able to anticipate up-coming scenes, the table collapsed—all four legs giving way at once—sending a dozen startled teenagers down in dusty implosion. The crowd roared its approval of this additional entertainment.

Xavier and Pascal agreed to run the film, by popular request, a third time. Barefooted, Franck, Fredy, Gilles and I left them to it, padding the now deserted streets of Jampea, our progress bathed in a blue lunar glow. The backdrop was two-dimensional, lush and cinematic, as if we'd entered a romantic jungle landscape painted by the German artist Walter Spies. That ill-fated fellow, I remembered, had died tragically in World War 2, a prisoner on the British ship transporting him from Bali for internment in Ceylon, when it was sunk by the Japanese. *And we're heading out into those same waters in a few days' time,* I couldn't help suppress a shudder.

We had earlier moved all our belongings aboard *Kurnia Ilahi*, in preparation for departure. Bruno had chosen to stay aboard and guard them all evening, armed with an oil lamp and machete, in case of thieves.

"I'll get the sampan," enthused Gilles, a big man with a generous soul, and a soft heart that sometimes led him into trouble. And he sloshed out blindly into the inky waters hoping to bump into our personal ferry, moored *somewhere* off this *approximate* section of shore, its painter anchored to a block of coral. His bear-like body was silhouetted by reflected silver, and plankton exploded angrily around his swashing legs, like lightning wrapped in cloud.

"Merde!" Pascal and Xavier caught up with us, tripping over unseen rocks in the intense darkness. Gilles hailed us from afar, invisible. We followed his voice, wading out until we bumped into his shadowy bulk, steadying the bobbing craft, the water up to our chests in the rising tide. He gave each of us a helpful shove over the side. When the five of us were settled inside the unstable craft, Xavier reached out, grabbed Gilles under the armpits, and hauled the last man in. In came Gilles ... and over turned the sampan.

And this was our *lifeboat*?

A LEAP OF FAITH

THE FADED BLUE *Jiefang* truck sat idling in a cloud of exhaust fumes. Sleepy-eyed Tibetan pilgrims clambered up the tailgate, hitching a free lift to Ganden Monastery, and I slipped in with them. Without a travel permit, it was the only way to get out of Lhasa, across the river, and past Chinese guards posted at all the city's entry and exit points. The pilgrims sensed my dilemma and gathered around, disguising me from casual inspection at the main checkpoint.

After about an hour, the transmission began to whine, the driver grinding down into first gear. He branched right, onto a rocky track, and began the slow ascent to the monastery.

Selecting a particularly tight hairpin bend, I leapt off the back of the lumbering vehicle, landing heavily and painfully on my hounded ankle. Friendly hands threw my backpack after me, and I limped downhill to the main road, turning right to follow the river valley, east.

On my own now, the enormity of what lay ahead hit home for the first time. But, once you have taken that first step, there can be no going back.

The road was empty. I sat for the next hour on my pack watching clouds scud past like puffy sails on an upturned ocean. Finally, I began to walk. This mere act of starting out seemed to summon up a truck. The driver slurred his vehicle to a halt a hundred yards beyond my waving hand. Alcohol fumes escaped when he opened the door to his cab. Still, it was a ride. And the thing you soon learned about hitchhiking was to be grateful for any chance of forward motion, no matter how dubious, uncomfortable or short-lived. One ride was organically connected to the next and to ignore the omens by, say, refusing a lift due to overly fussy or trivial concerns about personal safety, risked disturbing the entire balance of a Universe that had briefly aligned in order to transport you safely from A to B.

I knew what Claudia would say about my naïve and trusting fatalism, my talk of 'omens': she'd cast a cold, wet bucket of Teutonic realism all over them. Like the time when, back in Lhasa, I'd pointed out to her the sky, glowing such a brilliant red after sunset. I was sure it foretold of my making a successful trek to Chengdu:

"It's a sign!" I'd exclaimed in triumph.

"Idiot boy!" she'd brought me back down to earth: "That's the thing about signs. When you start looking for them, they pop up everywhere."

I was already missing Claudia, as though some vital part of my body had been amputated. I was acutely aware that she was planning to set off for Nepal later that same day, heading west as I went east. If only we could keep on going long enough in our opposing directions, and never give up faith, then surely our paths couldn't help but cross again?

Or had she forgotten about me as soon as I'd left, intent on getting back to her married lover?

READYING FOR DEPARTURE

IT WAS OUR last full day on Jampea. I wandered the fringe of the island, savoring the gritty, sun-warmed earth between my toes, the stability of a beach to lie on, and the reliable shade of the coconut groves: all the comforts I'd hitherto taken for granted and would be casting away from so soon, and so casually.

A bitter existential argument had broken out. We were in Sauda's house. His women cowered behind curtains and the men studied the glowing tips of their *kreteks* as European voices raged.

"What's the difference between crossing the Channel from Calais to Dover, and Jampea to Singapore, eh?" Pascal shouted at Fredy, who refrained from giving the literal answer: *About one thousand nine hundred and seventy miles. And sharks.* Peaceable, sensitive Fredy was the only one of us brave enough to stand up to moody Pascal. I soon found out what the problem was. Gaby, the weasel, had managed to get hold of both the sextant and the ship's compass. He was refusing to give up these essential instruments of navigation unless paid a higher commission.

"It is blackmail!" Pascal hissed, pained by the treachery of his handpicked mediator. "To 'ell with him. I refuse to pay for equipment I already own. He can keep it!"

"But, Pascal, be reasonable. We can't navigate all the way to Singapore without a compass," urged the butcher's son. The rest of us all agreed with Fredy's stance, though such was the force of Pascal's magnetism I knew I would get on that ship and set sail, even without the ransomed equipment. If Pascal said we'd arrive safely in Singapore, then who were we and the wind and the waves to disagree?

Looking back on it, there was nothing to stop the seven of us rushing Gaby and torturing the location of our gear out of him. He was hovering on the edge of the room half expecting us to, anyway, his flight instincts only marginally overshadowed by those of greed.

Normally, in Indonesia, sensitive discussions of payment were kept secret. If a man made twenty dollars, he'd tell you he received only ten, it being unwise to let family and friends — let alone any distant, unrelated government — know his true worth. Only a fool was transparent in matters of money. Knowing this, Xavier stepped in, and directly demanded the unspeakable of Gaby, in the packed parliament of Sauda's parlor.

"So, Gaby. How much do you want?"

All eyes turned to judge the shrinking Maumerian. He hadn't expected his infidelity to be exposed in such a public forum. In English, to avoid the figure's immediate calculation, he said:

"Two hundred thousand." About one hundred US dollars.

"No, no, way too high," smiled Xavier, all reason and charm, and then in Bahasa for all to hear:

"*Seratus Ribu*," he halved Gaby's demand to fifty dollars.

"Pah, keep it you cheat!" interjected Pascal, "You are not worth one hundred Rupiah."

Xavier persisted. "Come on Gaby, it is a fair price." The rest of us nodded and made agreeable noises. "It will come out of my

share, Pascal, don't worry," Xavier added. This seemed to get
through to Pascal, who calmed down. Gaby was quick to realise
he wouldn't get a better offer, and besides, he was starting to feel
the critical heat of Jampea public opinion turn against him.

"Okay, okay, one hundred thousand. Give me the money
outside, not in here." We agreed to his final face-saving
concession.

That evening, half the village crammed in to Sauda's homestead,
eager to partake in our leaving feast. According to Bugis tradition,
a goat had been slaughtered, its meat variously stewed, braised
and satéd in honor of our departure. *Pak* Sauda's womenfolk,
understandably proud of the result of all their hard work, were
in festive mood. Cigarette smoke billowed out from glassless
windows and was swept across Jampea Bay on the same reliable
breeze we hoped tomorrow would guide us safely to Singapore.

Ambo, whose natural instinct was to blend in, gecko-like with
the wallpaper, was prompted by whistles and catcalls to center
stage. He stood, hesitantly, muttered a few words and handed
to Pascal a beautifully detailed model boat, similar in style to
Kurnia Ilahi.

This tribute prompted Pascal to rise and deliver an
excruciatingly eloquent speech in flowery French — which
everyone pretended to understand and admire — and then we
toasted our safe passage to the distant Lion City with bottles of
sugary Sosro tea.

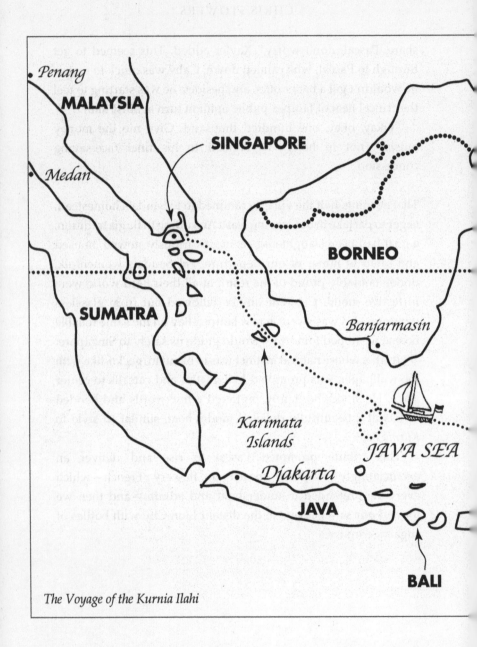

The Voyage of the Kurnia Ilahi

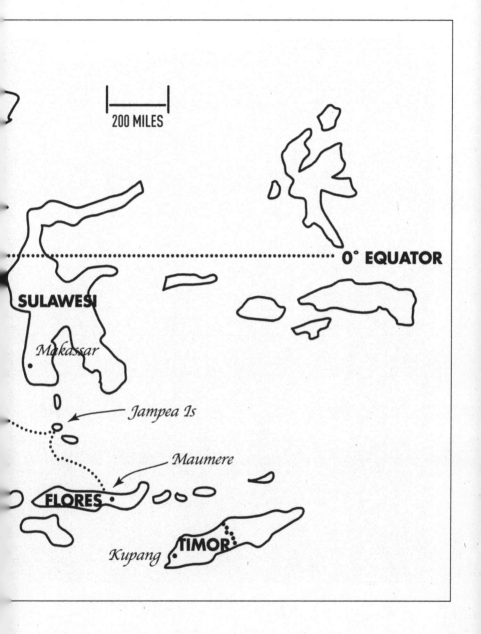

200 MILES

0° EQUATOR

SULAWESI

Makassar

Jampea Is

Maumere

FLORES

Kupang

TIMOR

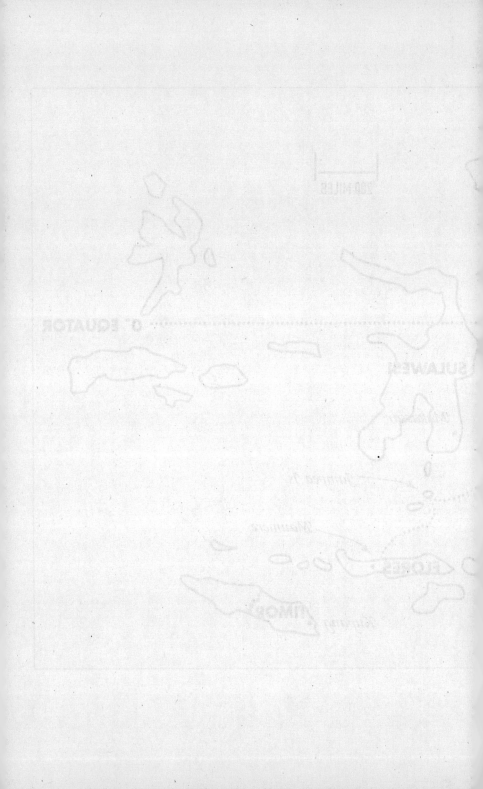

PART

3

THE VOYAGE
Kurnia Ilahi
Sunday, 11th September 1988

Voyage, Day 1
18:00 hrs: Approx. 20-miles from Jampea-Bearing 280/290°

I WAS IN too deep now to pull out of this mad venture. I wouldn't, even if I could have. I imagined the feeling being similar to that people had on the morning of their wedding. We were totally unprepared for the voyage, but both Pascal and Ambo agreed: *Kurnia Ilahi* had to set off immediately or it would be too late; the winds would change, whether we reached Singapore, or not.

Glad as I was that my Bartholomew's *Map of South East Asia,* that I'd purchased in Adelaide a few months earlier, was proving useful, I was somewhat taken aback it was the *only* such chart anyone had thought to bring along. We did have our recently retrieved floating compass, now nailed to the cabin and in clear line of sight of the helmsman. In addition, there were two oil lamps for signaling with, a wood fire stove for cooking on, and fresh water filling a huge 250-liter barrel lashed to the mast, and more in a number of jerry cans in the hold. Obviously, safety remained of the highest priority. Accordingly, we had the lifeboat – the small leak in its hull having been filled with chewing gum – five machetes with which to repel marauders, and the flags of three nations, stitched together by *Pak* Sauda's aged mother, ready to hoist at a moment's notice should proof of identity be required. These comprised the horizontal red and white stripes of Indonesia – nautical etiquette requiring this be flown whilst in her territorial waters – the French Tricoleur, naturally the largest of the three, and a small but complex 'Red Duster' (the red ensign used by British merchant ships since 1707) representing the British contingent. Fredy was peeved he didn't merit a flag of his own, but our budget was limited and, as Pascal reminded him, *you Swiss don't 'ave an ocean.*

What we also did *not* have – over-rated equipment such as radar, ship-to-shore radio, an engine, depth sounder, distress flares or lifejackets – was more than made up for by Pascal's secret weapon: the sextant. Or so he attempted to reassure us.

Franck, Fredy and I were dispatched with a fistful of Rupiah for a final sweep of Jampea's lively market place. We beached the sampan on a sandbank, tied it to some coral and waded in to shore, shoals of tiny blue fish darting around our ankles. On top of the usual list of essential items necessary to sustain us through a three-week voyage, we picked up seventy-seven young coconuts, a kilogram of sweet, black Bugis tobacco, and a dozen bottles of Bintang beer with which – optimistically – to celebrate crossing the equator. We had '280 eggs' written on our list, but there were only six dozen to be found in the entire market. So, we purchased all these, and three live chickens (and the grain to feed them), too.

Xavier was turning into Pascal's right-hand man, naturally enough, they being of similar age and balancing each other's temperaments. Pascal was all spit and sinew, whereas Xavier oozed suave confidence. Both men commanded natural authority.

I feared the erratic and volatile nature of Pascal; Xavier's mandate was supported by his effortless, worldly intelligence.

They rejoined the *Kurnia Ilahi*, delivered by the Harbor Master on his private motor sampan, having dealt with last-minute documentation: our Port of Exit papers from Jampea, and some Customs formalities. These 'formalities', judging by Pascal's mood, had cost quite a bit in 'tea money'. But his fury soon subsided. The breeze was strong and boded well for our voyage. Pascal was only ever happy escaping from a place.

A ramshackle flotilla of small craft approached us across the bay. Aboard, in prime position, perched *Pak* Sauda and Ambo, his two sons Ahmod and Achmed, the *Kepala Desa* – the village head man – in every single one of Indonesia's settlements, no matter how remote or insignificant, you will find such an official, and various village elders, trailed by an entourage of lower ranking family members and well-wishers. Pulling alongside the *Kurnia Ilahi*, they swarmed deftly aboard, curiously poking into every nook and cranny of the vessel, criticizing the deplorable state of our ropes and the lack of ballast in our hold. Young daredevils took turns diving into the crystalline waters from higher and higher up the rigging. Xavier was called upon to administer a last-minute *medicament* to the infected foot of *Pak* Hussein's youngest son. The policeman himself was looking a bit queasy, possibly the result of having overdone the nivaquine.

Mama Sauda offered around a huge tray piled high with sticky rice and coconut delicacies. We considered ourselves particularly honored by her presence, since the only time women were traditionally allowed to set foot on the deck of a *perahu* was after a white cock and a black goat had been ritually slaughtered in a 'leaving land' ceremony. In olden days, this auspicious date for setting sail would have been determined by the *bissu* – the transgendered village shaman. I figured that, having feasted on goat the night before, and bought the chickens — among them one white hen — in the market that very morning, we had ticked-off sufficient articles of Bugis folklore for the village elders to allow their women be loosed-upon our deck, prior to raising anchor.

I spied Gaby sitting alone, up on the prow, whittling away on a chunk of wood with his flick-knife. As reluctant as I was to revise my earlier assessment of his character, and unsure of what unfounded prejudices he still held against me for having left my hat behind in the room of his mistress, I had a request to make of him. It was a task that only Gaby — who was heading back to Flores directly after our departure — was in a position to fulfill.

"*Apa kabar*, Gaby?" I approached hesitantly. At my greeting he looked up, briefly, from his craftwork.

"*Mas* Chris, sit here. So, you are really going to sail with that madman Pascal? You are more crazy than you look!" said the self-admitted murderer, bringing me nicely to my point:

"In case we don't make it, Gaby, will you post this for me when you get back to Maumere?" I handed him a thick envelope addressed to Claudia in Bonn (the latest address I had for her), containing copied highlights of my diary entries all the way from Kupang to Jampea. It was a risk; I could lose them forever if Gaby decided to take the postage money and dump the letter. But that risk was ever so slightly outweighed right now by the distinct possibility that we'd sink before reaching Singapore.

"Of course! You can trust me," replied Gaby, as I knew he would, reaching out and grabbing both cash and letter at once. I was left not much reassured.

There followed a deferential hush, signaling a rare moment of seriousness. Ambo, a man of few words, bashfully stepped forward and presented Pascal with a beautiful antique machete, housed in an elaborately decorated sheath. This marked the symbolic hand over of the vessel, from one captain to another.

At two o'clock, and with final assistance from a couple of members of the *Kurnia's* original crew, we raised the mainsail halfway and pulled up the big anchor. *Kurnia Ilahi*, sensing her moment of freedom, strained lightly, starting to drag her remaining two anchors through the sand. The good people of Jampea scrambled back into their various canoes and launches; the men and boys waving, many of the women sobbing through their smiles.

A couple of the more brazen girls pretended to drag Fredy back with them. And for a moment his expression looked so set and serious I was certain he was going to jump ship. The urge to experience Paradise is great; but the idyll is ruined the moment we set foot on it. I felt a lump in my throat, and waved back furiously at the shrinking mass of arms, shouting out the lie that *I'll come back soon!*

I know I never will.

Fortunately, we had practical considerations to rescue us from the debilitation of nostalgia. Immediate among these was the sudden realization that, of the entire crew, only Pascal had ever sailed before. We were going to have to, quite literally, 'learn the ropes' as we went along. Bruno and Gilles busied themselves securing a thirty-meter length of rope to the poop deck, letting it trail the ship in case any of us fell overboard.

"I read about it in your 'Ornblower," Gilles happily admitted, obviously a fan—as was I—of C.S. Forester's fictional naval hero, Horatio Hornblower.

Xavier and Franck devised a rope and pulley system helping to ease the effort of steering the heavy teak rudder. Fredy erected a sunshield to protect the chickens, and began to figure out the flags. And Pascal approached me, with notebook and pencil.

"Here, Chris, you work out the rota, for our shifts." He meant for our turns at the tiller, the distribution of which would define the pattern and pace of our lives at sea for the next two weeks or more. I edged my way out on the prow; the roaring waters and wind in my hair helped concentrate thought:

KURNIA ILAHI/STEERING ROTA

NIGHT
Shift 1: 9 p.m. — 12 midnight
Shift 2: 12 midnight — 3 a.m.
Shift 3: 3 a.m. — 6 a.m.
DAY
Shift 4: 6 a.m. — 9 a.m.
Shift 5: 9 a.m. — 12 noon * sextant reading
Shift 6: 12 noon — 3 p.m.
Shift 7: 3 p.m. — 6 p.m.
Shift 8: 6 p.m. — 9 p.m.

A day divided naturally enough into eight three-hour watches. That these would be further split between the elements of darkness and of light entertained a certain Brechtian appeal. Obviously, night shifts would be the most arduous, necessitating two crew on duty, at all times. Whilst the others slept, their lives would be in the hands of one man at the helm — unable to see clearly over the cabin in front of him — and his watch partner, up on the prow, alert for any random objects, such as stray shipping and islands, wishing to collide with us.

The daytime portion contained two additional watches, and since most of us would be awake then, only one person would be required on duty at the tiller. There being five day shifts and six crewmen (Pascal, as captain, refused to tie himself down with any such workman-like involvement), we could alternate these, allowing one of us out of a shift every day. I staggered the night shifts so that we worked different watches and changed partners every third day. Since the first night watch was already upon us, I elected to test the model, and shared the tiller with Fredy.

The sheer number and variety of nautical terms littering the English language has always taken me aback. This was naïve and untutored of me, considering the long and profitable love affair my island nation has enjoyed with the sea. Take 'taken aback', for example. Who but the saltiest of seadogs would have imagined this common-day expression emerged as the result of an inattentive helmsman allowing the wind to blow backward into his sheets, causing a sudden shift in the position of the boom? I was reminded, belatedly, of the maritime wisdom of my ancestors when the wind, gusting directly from behind, caught the flapping port side of the mainsail as we strayed a few degrees off course, down a swell.

The deck plunged; the great boom whipped across the top of the cabin, and tormented ropes splintered the rear of the poop deck. Franck and Bruno, who were sleeping under the stars, went with it, pushed like pennies in a seaside arcade game. The tiller creaked alarmingly as I fought to keep us on course, the deck tilting steeply, pulling the stern upwards. Pascal, lapsing into French "*Attention, attention!*" warned of dangerously swinging pulley blocks and a confusion of heavy objects skidding across the slippery deck. We managed, with all hands, to force the boom back to its original side. *Kurnia* settled back down, and we decided to continue on using only the jib whilst making a damage assessment.

Luckily Franck and Bruno could be accounted for, having fallen onto the narrow deck, rather than shooting over it, into the sea.

Amid the adrenaline rush, one of our hens had laid the first egg of the voyage.

Readings and Repairs

Day 2
18:00 hrs: Approx. 130-miles from Jampea-Bearing 285°

I FOCUSED ON my watch face through sleep-filled eyes. Its drooping arms indicated the time was 5:30 a.m. Out beyond the cabin, a young sun pushed through the horizon like an inflamed zit on the face of a hormonal teenager. Bruno, framed by the cabin doorway, was leaning on the tiller; very possibly napping. Stumbling around and past him in order to pee off the poop deck, I was shocked to see only sea. Then I remembered where I was and what we were attempting to do, and decided it best to go and brew a pot of tea. Along with a mug from this, I ate two Bugis cakes in preparation for my shift at the helm. We still were being tailed by an annoying backwind and were riding some large swells, sailing a watery corridor between two storm fronts. We were making maybe six knots; compass bearing swinging between 270-300°.

And then it happened. We crested a swell, and a huge trough opened up like a valley beneath us. The ship launched into a crazy surf down this wall of milky green sea. The rudder

7777

77777

77777

was powerless to prevent *Kurnia* veering off course, the wind grabbing at her sail and jerking the boom across the cabin like a monstrous windscreen wiper. There was a loud explosion as the boom snapped from its joint with the mast. My sleepy-eyed crewmates rushed to pull the big sheet down, and *Kurnia* righted herself. Meanwhile, I was being flung back and forth across the deck, battling to rein in the tiller, wrenching my knee and scraping the skin off my left shin in the process. I tried to keep the boat pointing into the wind. A further freak gust loosened the boom, sending the heavy bamboo pole crashing down into the water, the flapping sheet fleeing behind it like a startled ghost.

Without pausing to think — *the man has guts* — Pascal dived after it, over the side and onto the submerged sail, which now resembled a wild, sinking paddling pool which threatened to be sucked under the keel, tilting the boat over on its way. A manic grin broke across his unshaven face. He yelled out some words, eaten by the wind, though Franck, closer to him, seemed to understand. Dashing back into the cabin he returned with the ceremonial machete, which he tossed down to our captain. Pascal used this to hack at the tangle of ropes, managing to free the boom and, after much straining and cursing, we manhandled both the heavy bamboo boom and sodden sail onboard. We were only two days out of Jampea. What else was going to go wrong?

Sailing with just the jib, pitching and rolling with the waves, we were able to return to a course of around 260°, though moving much slower through the water due to our now reduced acreage of sail. We would, no doubt, soon get the hang of all these ropes and pulleys, but predicting the whims of a fickle sea would take much longer. Fredy suggested an early lunch. Xavier and I sliced up sweet potatoes — our supply of which, along with all the bananas, were ripening nicely in the hold — for the cook's pot.

Meanwhile, the detached boom presented a technical

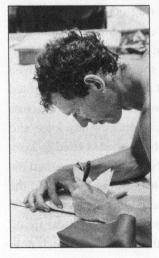

Pascal

challenge. Since it comprised a single length of giant bamboo, Pascal, with Fredy advising, decided simply to saw-off one complete joint—about two-feet in length—and reattach the stunted version to the mast joint. The carpentry, and the replacement of slashed ropes, took until 11:45 a.m., when, taking a break and posing dramatically, his legs astride the cabin rooftop and silhouetted against a pale blue sky, Pascal began to take preliminary sextant readings, in the run-up to noon.

1:15 p.m.: *Pascal is still studying the charts and calculating our latitude.*

2:30 p.m.: *He's now in a rage.*

Pascal blamed these confused calculations on the nautical almanac he'd brought along, which, he said, contained only data for readings taken in the *northern* hemisphere (hardly the book's fault, but I wasn't going to add to our captain's frustration, and growing anger, by pointing this out). Additionally, he may have been confusing his northern and southern hemispheres with the sun being north or south of the equator, and whether to add or subtract the declination of the sun in his calculations. And that was before throwing in height-of-eye corrections to account for how far he was standing above sea level whilst taking those readings. Basically, he had no idea where we were.

The sea is just a watery desert. With no cover between us and the sun, the afternoon heated up quickly, and without mercy. We rigged a spare rectangle of sail material across the poop deck to keep the worst of the solar rays off of the helm. The wind had, mercifully, changed direction by now, and was blowing steadily from the southeast. We could risk raising the mainsail to its fullest extent. Despite much creaking, the boom repairs seemed to hold. *Kurnia* stretched out luxuriously, like a cat, leaning into the waves a few degrees, and we skipped along at a jaunty five or six knots. *This* was what sailing was all about! Xavier soon assembled his Walkman and speakers. The rear deck became bathed by the melodies of a British group Franck introduced me to, *The Pale Fountains*. And we played *The Waterboys* 'Don't Bang the Drum' over and over.

This was fast becoming the soundtrack to our voyage.

That evening, using my own version of Haji Baju's trusted dead-reckoning system, I attempted to calculated our current watery location. From the approximate number of hours we had been moving, and the estimated speed during each of those hours, to the rough compass headings we had followed, and the amount of time we held each of these, I arrived at the educated, and entirely random, conclusion that we were a hundred and thirty miles from Jampea, and seventy miles southwest of Makassar. This intersection I dotted with a biro, marking our *official* progress across my Bartholomew's map.

Dreams and Drudgery

"Claudia ... mmm ... claudia," I moaned in ecstasy as she expertly massaged the tight knots in my neck. What a lovely way to wake up. I remembered peering up into her beady eyes, seeing her pink snout, just a blur at such close range. Her whiskers, short and bristly, caressed my cheek: "You need a shave," I heard myself advising.

Shave? Snout? The pig squealed away in fright as I sprang upright. A Tibetan herdsman sat on a rock by the cave entrance, unmoved, as though coming across itinerant Europeans was an everyday occurrence in these parts. He smiled, spat out a chewed twig, and carried on staring as though waiting for the next act to begin.

I'd been on the road from Lhasa for ten days, and was covering progressively fewer miles in each of them. My spirits slumped as the number of trucks passing by decreased — I'd seen four vehicles *all day*, yesterday — and none of them had stopped. Walking was becoming a trial; my clothes were eternally damp from all the rain and the sweat, and a red welt of fleabites and friction sores now banded my torso and was beginning to travel up and down both arms and legs. On the plus side, I was getting used to trudging under the heavy backpack. I set a pace according to the telegraph poles. Twenty-two poles marked each kilometer, eighty paces per pole. I made up a chant to help me get from one pole to the next:

> Something will come along.
> Something always does. If you're
> Not too fussy about what
> That something is.
> Don't complain, 'coz one day, way in the future,
> Something will not come along.
> The Universe will shudder; the dots will fail
> To connect.
> That day is the beginning of the end.
> Put it to the back of your mind.
> It is still a long way off.

Last night I'd hit a low point and been reduced to sleeping in a cave. Now, on its own, a cave is not a bad place to rest ones' head, and I'd been content to be sleeping outdoors, my lungs filled with fresh country air, on a bed of straw. I'd lulled myself to sleep considering the old conundrum of how cruel it is the young rarely have enough money to enjoy their youth, the middle-aged are denied the time to appreciate their wealth, and the elderly haven't the health to enjoy either. My life would be for naught if I didn't at least attempt to shatter this cynical template.

Then I'd woken, scratching, in the middle of the night, and discovered the main function of the grotto was as a stock-pen for sheltering herds, and that my thin skin and fresh blood were providing an irresistible and exotic addition to the menu for hundreds of their fleas and ticks.

The next day, while refilling my canister with drinking water at one of the numerous, roadside springs—making sure to first sterilize the dubious, brownish liquid with iodine pills—a tanned Tibetan peasant latched on to me. We ambled along in amiable silence. His long, greasy, greying locks escaped from beneath a crumpled hat, and his body was encased in a stinking fleece pulled together by a length of rope at the waist. He mimed a desire to share my food, and we divided up my final packet of biscuits.

This region, around Bomi, had long attracted such pilgrims and free spirits; seekers of the prophesized *beyul*—a Tibetan *El Dorado*—said to lie within its borders. It was believed the ancient dynasty of first Tibetan kings came from Bomi's Yarlung Valley, and the whole region—rather like its Pakistani counterpart, Hunza—had been a semi-independent kingdom until forcefully integrated into the greater Tibetan empire at the start of the 20th century.

I felt sure that, could we have secured a common language, my new companion would have let me—a complete stranger and fellow nomad—in on his deepest and most tragic tales. In this world of transient souls, the mightiest were those who risked criticism and braved vulnerability. *To the nomad, every day is a sentimental parting and arrival. The settled never bother to unpack their emotions.*

Marching on fewer than a thousand calories a day, I was fading away, fast. I'd also developed a worrying cough: a deep evacuation of phlegm and blood coming from the bottom of my lungs. I put this down to the altitude, and the dust. My ankle wound was looking angry and inflamed, so I avoided looking at it. Truth be told, I hardly felt it. It was like hunger: always there, gnawing away, relentless, just another annoyance to be shoved behind the mental wall.

At twilight, I wordlessly infiltrated the encampment of a group of bedraggled Tibetan pilgrims who were sitting in a circle, at the edge of a long, placid lake. Its surface was a darkened mass, threatening to absorb all remaining light. Here they brewed-up yak butter tea in their soot-blackened kettle, and passed around chunks of *tsampa*, bullet-sized pellets of roughly ground barley flour, mixed in the palm of the hand with yak butter, which we chewed on, raw.

The day ended in much the same manner as it had begun, scratching at fleabites, fighting back stomach cramps and waves of dysentery. A little closer to Chengdu, still lost to the world; yet, oddly, in no hurry to be found.

> *Dreams and reality merge on a clear Himalayan night.*
> *I wake, disorientated by stars.*
> *My hands sink into the soil,*
> *Clawing for purchase.*
> *I lie suspended above a bottomless astral ocean.*
> *I have only to release my grip,*
> *And I'd plunge straight in.*
> *My body would leave no ripple.*

Going Bananas

BRUNO SHOOK ME awake at the end of his shift. It was 3 a.m., though day and night had lost all meaning by now. There was just steering or sleep, happy or scared, hot or wet: usually a combination of all the above. He poured me coffee from the thermos and Gilles surrendered his place at the tiller, pointing out the two stars he'd been trusting to bear us on a course of 285°. They disappeared inside the low cabin, and Fredy and I were left in charge.

My world is small.

4 a.m., and all was dark. Fredy was on lookout, up at the prow, leaving me at the helm. My practical universe was reduced to the proportions of a Neolithic cave, its dimensions dictated by the flickering arc of a paraffin lamp. *Kurnia Ilahi* was enveloped by stars; it was as though we were caught inside a gigantic nocturnal snow globe that had just been given a healthy shake. Astral bodies were sent shooting into the heavens, and then settled down, sinking through the oceans' mirror. I rolled a cigarette using a few strands of sweet, black Bugis tobacco, and

inhaled its strong, honeyed incense, infused, like all our supplies now, with the tang of sea salt. *Kurnia* dipped and rose, carried by gentle, hypnotic swells. I sat cross-legged on her worn teak planks, arm resting on the tiller, feeling her tug a suggested course, and concentrating on alignment with the two stars, keeping one on either side of the second line to the mast.

This shift, from 3 a.m. to 6 a.m., was the most magical. Beginning in the hour of nights' deepest despair, it ended with rebirth, at dawn. I lowered a bucket into the sea and showered in salt water, droplets sparking molten gold in the sun's young rays. Dolphins kept us company; playing with us, taunting our lack of speed and grace, corkscrewing beneath the keel to emerge in glistening arcs, far on the other side of the ship.

My world is small. But my horizon is limitless.

Our load of bananas began to ripen all at once, twenty bunches of the things. These were no ordinary bananas; the fruits of Jampea were each over twelve inches long. Fredy spent most of his watch by the stove, at the base of the mast, thinking up new ways to present them. Banana pancakes were his latest wheeze, using eggs and rice flour for the batter. Then there were his banana fritters *a la Bernaise* — fried in coconut oil with flour, brown sugar and peanuts — fresh bananas, stewed bananas, banana porridge, banana salad and banana split (a fresh banana, split in two, the halves dunked in condensed milk). We had to resist digging into any of the less perishable foodstuffs, leaving them until later in the voyage.

When not on duty steering or carrying out essential tasks of repair, or cooking, or manning the bilge pump, I would dive into the cabin, collapse my bruised frame onto the three-foot by six-foot section of hardwood planking that had been designated as

Fredy

'mine', and fall instantly asleep. Normally it would take a pretty vigorous shake from one of my crewmates to rouse me from this deathly slumber, but today panicked shouting was sufficient to snap me out of my dreams—shouting, and being thrown to the far side of the cabin—as the *Kurnia Ilahi* tilted wildly on a freak wave. I staggered out on deck, my nerves relaxing a little at the sight of the others rushing about, gathering up fallen sheets of sail in their arms, but most definitely *not* abandoning ship. I soon identified the culprit: the rope holding aloft the entire mainsail had snapped. This, well, all of our ropes really, were among the many items Pascal had said he was going to renew *when we get to Singapore*. That was *if* we ever got to Singapore. For now, though, we were stalled, bobbing like a cork and pointing back toward Jampea.

Pascal, belonging to that tough Norman breed who only really come alive in times of adversity, swiftly sized up our dilemma. He tied our last fresh rope around his waist and started up the mast on the flimsy ladder, regardless of the several rungs this was missing. Its surviving rungs were crudely nailed to vertical poles designed to support a Bugis half his size and weight. The mast swung back and forth like a metronome. We craned our necks and squinted into the dizzying midday sun. Sixty feet above the deck, Pascal freed the jammed pulley and threaded the new rope. Then he descended, splinters from the rough ladder frame slicing into his hands, and attached the end of the rope to the collapsed upper boom. Back on solid deck he immediately jammed himself in the shrouds, and vomited over the rail.

"*Merde. Quelle kamikaze!*" he panted, grinning, his eyes flashing a suggestion of ancestral blood lust.

We were all a bit on edge. The one constant factor in this voyage, *Kurnia Ilahi,* was falling apart. I waded through a depth of two feet of sea water in the bilge when harvesting bananas for our evening meal; it reminded me we needed to re-caulk the hull in Singapore, too. Up on deck, Gilles attempted to open a coconut with a machete. At least our first aid kit was relatively extensive, and until now, untested. The unexpected cry of seagulls, as we sailed blindly into another night, was more worry than relief. They signaled that land must be nearby; and where there was land, sandbanks and reefs. Only there *were* no islands shown on my map.

Either the birds were lost, or we were.

CHARLY

I HAVEN'T FORGOTTEN about Charly. He's integral to this story, and yet remains separate from it: both an enigma, and as an agent for change. When I'd bumped in to him, alighting the plane in Kupang, it hadn't been surprise I'd felt, so much as anticipation. Adventure was in the air, and I felt sure I was to be the major recipient of the coming disruptions Charly always seemed to herald. In Tibet, as in Timor, I always had the impression I was slowing him down, that he could travel onwards much faster alone. Certainly, the fact that he pursued life at a more furious pace than most was a crucial factor to our ever having met in the first place. It was, in fact, what Claudia had been banking on.

"I can recommend ze mutton noodles," a deep voice rasped from behind me in the rickety food hut, making me jump. I'd set off from Lhasa to Chengdu twelve days earlier, and had encountered only Tibetans and Chinese, the entire time. This was as far off the grid as I'd ever been. Indeed, it took me a while to process the tones that had been spoken, and even longer to compute that they were in English and, furthermore, that I could understand them. What he said next really shocked me:

"You must be Chris." The tall, gangly Frenchman thrust out

a hand and we shook, polite protocol becoming more important the further you find yourself from home. "I'm Charly," he announced, "I 'ave a letter for you, oh, and some medicine. From Claudia."

As he began rummaging for pills in his canvas sack — the type that sailors take on shore leave — I unfolded Claudia's handwritten note. This was all too much: one moment I had been alone and lost to the world, the next I was found, and gifts were being bestowed.

My Dear Idiot Boy,

If you are reading this, then Charly will have caught up with you, and you will have not yet died of rabies. You will also learn that I have reached Nepal. Well done to both of us!

How I wished you would have come with me to Kathmandu ... but instead you had to set off and follow your fate in a different direction. It will not be easy, this route you have chosen in life, but I sense you can travel no other way.

Unless he has used them on himself first, then accept these pills I gave to Charly as my gift to you. The chemist here said they work wonders. Or did he wonder if they'd work? Anyway, I suspect you have few other options, so for once listen to the advice of your (not so much) elders, and swallow the verdammt things!

As we get older, we meet fewer significant people, we are shocked and amused by less and protect ourselves under ever thickening layers of cynicism and practicality. Thank you for breaking through, to touch me, as I hope I have been able to touch you.

When I get back to Germany I shall be moving from Munich to Bonn. Government work, my Dear, super hush-

hush. Worry not: there will always be a plate of Weisswurst
and crate of Augustiner Helles in my kitchen should you
decide to pay a visit. You can take the girl out of Bavaria,
after all … just don't try depriving her of real food!
    Deine Claudia XXX

PS. This coming winter, or next, I plan to travel to South
East Asia. It is a big place, but keep an eye out for me – as I
shall be doing for you …

Charly had bumped into Claudia the day she'd arrived in
Kathmandu, exhausted after her trek which had been beset by
heavy rains and landslides. Despite this, she had immediately
rushed out to buy some antibiotics and charged Charly with
them, telling him to travel as fast as he could in order to overtake
me, *en route*. Triumphantly, he pulled out a plastic tray containing
red and grey capsules.

"*Ici, voila!* Amoxyl. 'Ere, *mon ami*. You can find all kinds of
shit in zose Nepalese pharmacies!" Charly winked, "I 'ave some
valium, too, and zese yellow ones … I 'ave no idea what zey are
for. If yours don't work, just ask. There's plenty to go around."

It was the faintest of chances—yet those were the ones that
appeared to be enjoying most success at the time—and it had
taken Charly a mere six days to catch up with me from Lhasa.
I thought, guiltily, about having deserted Claudia. We could
have been together now, doing the normal stuff that travelers
do. Enjoying exotic food and clean sheets. But whichever way
I had gone, I would have bumped into this gregarious, bearded
Frenchman. Charly was twenty-five, languid and calm. Nothing
seemed to faze him. Until last month he'd been working at a
nuclear power facility in Grenoble. They'd refused him leave to
travel, so he'd quit and flown straight to India. He hadn't stopped

moving since, focused on his objective of getting to Australia. I admired his determination, but questioned his command of geography:

"Eet is not about traveling in a straight line, *mon ami*. *Non*. Eet is ze challenge of man against nature. Ze tougher ze road, ze more eet makes me want to take eet. Besides, I 'ave not much money, and China is very cheap." And to economize, he'd moved in to my room.

"*Merde*. Zat looks like shit!" he exclaimed when, later, I took off my boots and socks and began to tend to my suppurating wound in a bucket of tepid water. "It *smells* like shit, too." Without the benefit of alternant opinion, I'd just grown used to it. "Doesn't it 'urt?"

"Not really. Claudia must have told you about the dog biting me in Lhasa? I guess I'm just waiting for it to go away. Or something else ..." A something else I was unwilling to think about, for that way led to defeat.

Maybe it was me that was jinxed? Instead of carrying on at the faster pace Charly had hitherto been setting, we seemed to slow down to mine. The 5 a.m. truck wasn't there, so we walked back to our tomb-like hotel along the deserted main street, picking up stones to ward off dogs. Daylight brought with it renewed hope, the sun's rays acting as a natural memory-wiping device. It helped us to battle the absence of hope that overwhelms the desperate hours of darkness. With morning light and coffee, I could take on the world.

"Freshly ground beans from Indochine, ze Bolovens plateau, *arabica*," Charly had fantasized.

"For me, a cappuccino, with double, no, *triple* shot of espresso," I countered. It was our game, attempting to keep hunger at bay by dreaming of the extravagances we'd indulge in once we made it out of Tibet. It was an act of masochism. The only 'café' in the settlement was a truck stop serving *chaang* and omelettes laden with vicious little green-bullet chilies to a thin and irregular stream of passing truck drivers.

"Croissants, straight out of ze oven. With jam," Charly upped the stakes.

I squished and molded a two-day old lump of cold *tsampa* between my fingers and popped an amoxyl. Charly winced sipping at his glass of tepid tea, the color of urine.

Reality sucked.

A Kind of Mutiny

Day 4
18:00 hrs: Approx. Long. E 117°/Lat. S 6°-Bearing 285°

THE SHIP'S CABIN was a three-foot high afterthought, tacked on top of the main deck: it offered slightly less shelter and comfort than a Himalayan cave. Emerging from the cracks and crevasses of its rough plank decking this morning swarmed a new breed of Baygon-resistant super cockroach. I think I preferred Tibetan fleas. These roaches were massive and aggressive; one bit my toe, awakening me for the start of the midnight shift.

Midnight to 3 a.m. was the worst time to be on duty: a bad dream endured between periods of blissful blackout. The sea was surging, creating the largest swells of the voyage yet. I started to imagine each plunge to be our last, yet somehow *Kurnia* always rose again. A lake, two-and-a-half feet deep was now sloshing around in the bilge, acting as an ever-shifting ballast. If we took on much more seawater we could capsize. As soon as the sun came up, Pascal assembled us and designated a parallel rota of shifts on the manual bilge pump. It was quite a workout, pumping the roughly-hewn wooden shaft, up and down for periods of twenty minutes each, over the course of the next six hours. My palms were blistered by noon.

We were on duty for eighteen-hours each day, fueled by bananas, sweet tea and Bugis cake. You'd think seven grown men enduring such close confinement would resort to confrontation, a battle of the egos; but our tempers didn't flare. Like prisoners in a chain gang, we had an unavoidable task to do and were just too tired, unnerved and undernourished to bother with passion.

Braced against the heaving deck, I cursed the stove as it stubbornly failed to ignite. Sea spray had dampened our firewood. I doused the small pile of twigs at the base of the stove with paraffin, but this only produced a thick, acrid smoke, and no heat. It was taking an age to boil the water for our morning coffee. I was enveloped in wood smoke. It clawed into my eyes and reminded me of Claudia. The passing sea and waves blurred in my peripheral vision and my mind began to wander. Travel can only really be experienced alone like this, allowing our thoughts to meld with an abstract, moving landscape. It is essential to empty our minds of clutter, so that again we can begin to focus. Increasingly, I felt at ease only in motion. It was not wasting time; I was going *somewhere*, even if it was just around in circles. I woke up from this reverie, my eyes smarting and dampened, and boiling water burbling from the spout of the kettle. It was obvious that either Claudia or I needed to stop traveling long enough for one of us to catch up with the other.

Meanwhile, the rest of the crew had been battling to bring the mainsail down and, with needle and thick thread, set about stitching up the rips made in the fabric overnight.

"*Attention!*" A huge wave caught us off guard, toppling over one of our jerry cans: all that precious drinking water. I made a dive for it, grabbing the plastic handle before the container slid over the edge. Half its contents were lost. In the ensuing ninety-minute struggle to raise the mainsail we also lost both our thermos flasks and an oil lamp (luckily there was a spare). Bruno received a gash on his forehead from the boom: blood was drawn. Finally, the sail went up, and forward character and purpose were once again restored to the *Kurnia Ilahi*. Soon we were racing up to six, possibly seven knots, the vessel's deck tensing and shuddering as we surged through dark grey crests, gripping white-knuckled to any available rope or rail on this relentless rollercoaster ride.

Flying fish shot across the deck, a shower of silvery javelins. Some hit the cabin in mid-flight. Fredy wanted to fry them up. I snatched a couple to bait a nail we had attached to a long thread and left dragging through the water, hoping to lure a more substantial catch. Monotony of diet was the problem, all these bananas. I was constipated. This condition led to worried minutes crouched on the *Kurnia's* 'toilet', a frail extension of planks secured by ropes to the back of the appropriately named 'poop deck'. Below, a long and contemplative drop into the sea: overhead, the red and white Indonesian flag, snapping in the breeze. I strained in time with the plunging waves.

At 5 p.m., Gilles called out from the fore. He had spotted a local boat, its sails furled, bobbing dramatically. This was the first vessel we'd seen, in all the watery vastness, since leaving Jampea behind. We came around to a southerly course, taking the wind out of our sails and reducing our speed to almost a standstill. Through Xavier's underpowered 8x30 magnification binoculars we scanned the little vessel for signs of distress.

"Make ready the machetes," Pascal warned. It was not just fish that were tempted by bait.

Thirty minutes passed. The other vessel made no attempt to signal us, in fact there was no sign of life on her decks at all. We turned back to our original course, soon picking up speed, and

eager to distance ourselves from all bad omens before darkness
settled-in.

Day 5
18:00 hrs: Approx. Long. E 115°/Lat. S 5°-Bearing 275°

CLOUD COVER SABOTAGED our attempt to navigate by the stars
tonight. Gilles and I took turns on the tiller and as lookout,
finding time passed faster if we swapped roles every half an
hour. Boiling up some water in the kettle, I discovered cracks
in two more of the jerry cans roped afore. All the precious fresh
water had drained out of them.

At dawn, the horizon thickened. Land! We drifted along,
expectant and excited at the first sight of *terra firma* in five days.
Five days, during which interval we may as well have become
the sole survivors of some Biblical flood, fated to drift on *Kurnia
Ilahi* until exhausted of all our supplies. Talking of religious
intervention, this seemed, to me, a Heaven-sent opportunity to
pull in and source some new ropes, maybe some water: *We're low
on tobacco, too,* warned Gilles, our main consumer of the black
weed. I mentioned the possibility to Pascal, and was surprised
when he agreed to try. We were almost parallel to the islands
now: both wind and current favoring such a maneuver.

The jib alone hadn't the strength to turn us, so we rehashed
an old and splintered rope, rushed it through the pulley block
and managed to raise the mainsail halfway before the ropes'
plastic sinews snapped completely, sending the sheet tumbling
to the deck. The island, close enough now to define several dark

contours along its southern flank, drifted further astern. Fate rarely dispatches its messengers of hope singly, and sure enough, a small, motorized fishing boat soon heaved into view. Jumping up and down wildly on top of the cabin, we shouted, waved our arms about and whistled to attract the attention of its crew. I used my shaving mirror to flash sunlight in their direction. The vessel spotted us, and changed course.

It was a local boat, the crew clad in sarongs, their heads protected by Muslim prayer caps. Pascal said he'd go with them to their island, and Fredy elected to accompany him. The Swissman's command of the Indonesian language was much the better of the two, so he'd come in handy as a translator. But I suspected, mainly, he wanted to keep an eye on Pascal.

"Water, vegetables, rope, paraffin, tobacco, firewood... grab all you can! Oh, and don't forget to find out what the island is called!" I shouted across to Fredy as the boats separated. It would be nice to discover where we actually were.

Both time and current meandered, dazed by the airless punishment of the tropical midday, on into the furnace of the afternoon. Xavier suggested lowering an anchor to keep us from losing sight of the island, but either the waters were too deep, or our rope of insufficient length. We kept on drifting.

Just as you have to force yourself to keep hydrated at altitude, so, in this heat, you had to continue to eat. We mechanically spooned Franck's lunchtime attempt at scrambled egg past our chapped and swollen lips. We had lost around thirty eggs today, smashed by the jarring deck, others having gone off. Not only had our hens become rather quiet of late, they hadn't been laying any replacement eggs, either. *Do chickens suffer seasickness?* Belatedly, I rued not adding 'eggs' to the list of supplies I'd shouted to Fredy, earlier.

Finally, at around 4 p.m., Fredy and Pascal arrived back in

the fishing launch. There was obvious tension between them. I took Fredy aside, when we were out of earshot of the others, up by the prow. Needless to say, they'd neglected to bring back any essential supplies.

"They asked for 500,000Rp. just to tow *Kurnia* to their island. 'Kramian', by the way: that's its name. You know what Pascal's like when he thinks he's being ripped off! He laughed at them, told them he would only pay 50,000Rp." Fredy stared out to sea, absently coiling a section of snapped rope around his forearm, between thumb and elbow.

"They said they would take us back to *Kurnia Ilahi* for that much. We had no choice. But just now Pascal stiffed them, only paying 30,000Rp. I think we should to be careful not to make any enemies out here…"

I instinctively subscribed to Fredy's Swiss cautiousness, and was glad for his help in pinpointing our present location. Whilst I had calculated the latitude pretty much spot-on, we'd travelled farther west than I ever imagined. We were only sixty miles south of Banjarmasin, where the Said sisters I'd met in Brisbane — guiding their school group at Expo88 — lived.

"Maybe, Fredy, we could head there? Our water is unlikely to last until Singapore, and god knows we could do with some new ropes and sail."

We, the *Kurnia Ilahi's* non-invested, non-French contingent, were aware of our lowly position in matters of social ranking. Only the chickens were below us. At the pinnacle of the dictatorial pyramid sat Pascal, amid the plump cushions and ermine, wielding absolute power. We, the plebs, suggested putting the possibility of a port call to popular vote. The word "mutiny" only entered my mind in retrospect, when I came to write this page.

Let it be recorded that:

- Those in favor of making a stopover to re-provision in Banjarmasin: Franck, Fredy and Chris.
- Those against: Xavier, Gilles and Bruno. And Pascal.
- There being no abstentions.
- Court rules in favor of continuing on present reckless and ruinous course to Singapore. May God — or his closest representative on earth, Pascal — help us all.

The decision out of my hands, I felt an unexpected wave of relief sweep through my body: *if we are to die on this voyage, it's not my fault.*

Following this day of high drama, we were gifted an evening of exceptional calm, onboard and at sea. I baked sweet potatoes on the open fire; Pascal, in conciliatory mood now, joyfully scrambled the remainder of our eggs and fried some banana pancakes; we consumed sweet coffee and played cards lulled by low swells, the sky aflame with the pyrotechnic wonder of an equatorial sunset. The scent of Gilles's cigarette smoke infiltrated the cabin as we sailed slowly, relying on the jib. Steering was light; I had only to lean into the smoothed wooden arm to correct *Kurnia* when she strayed past a bearing of 300°, soothing her back down to our preferred vector of 280°. I felt secure on this deck, at this task. The ship's various creaks and groans took on now the comforting liturgy of prayer. A port was an alien abstraction, an unwanted intrusion.

Kurnia Ilahi is our homeland now.

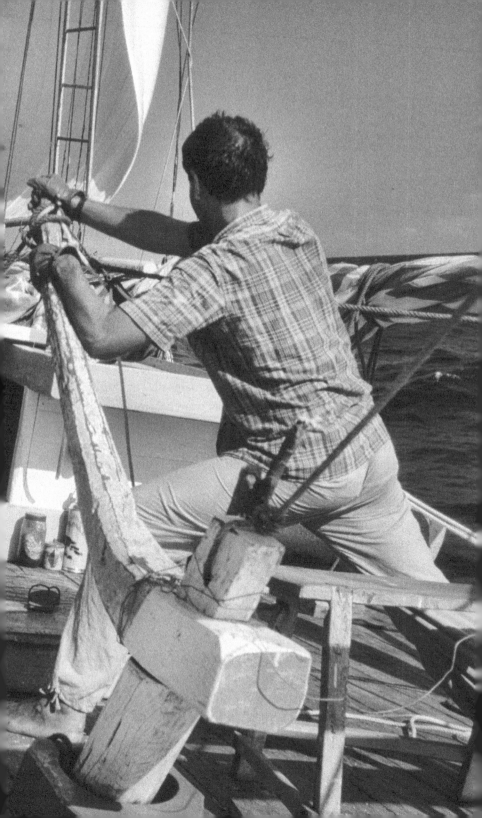

Day 6
18:00 hrs: Approx. Long. E 114°/Lat. S 5°-Bearing 280°

To PORT, LIGHTNING struck through the elemental ink at some unseen shore, and dolphins kept pace with us, their fins an explosion of electric green plankton. I sung quietly to myself the old nautical aide memoire: 'There's a little port left in the bottle. Port is on the left.'

Crackling into life, the AM radio on Xavier's Walkman picked up evidence of an alternative universe, the *muzzenin* call to prayer, from Madura, perhaps, or Surabaya. We were making a gentle four knots using only the jib; better this, than to risk snapping all our ropes at a faster pace with the mainsail. The Bugis cakes had almost run out, and the bananas were becoming slushy. So, for breakfast, I invented a "banana milkshake" — banana mush mixed with powdered and condensed milk, brown sugar and a freshly lain egg — it seemed to gain approval. Without condensed milk we would *have* no voyage.

I'll whisper it here for fear of offending the gods: *we've not had any emergencies today.* Franck and I carried on with our documentary work. I posed Pascal, along with his wristwatch and the sextant, for a photo near the compass, noting how it was 6 p.m., and not yet dark.

"We've moved into another time zone," he said. It was Java time now.

Purpose and destination: empowered by these fundamental elements, Man marks history and builds empires; he dreams. The wind; a wooden ship; hope of a distant horizon: this collection of improbable fantasies sets him free. Denied them, he is lost, his deeds and achievements go unrecorded. He becomes just another rock in the desert being eroded of all character by the timeless passing Mistral.

Nobody knew where I was. I sure as Hell didn't. But that was the beauty of it, and the danger. What possible alternative could there be—stagnation?

Nah, I'll leave that until retirement.

Day 7
18:00 hrs: Approx. Long. E 113°/Lat. S 4°-Bearing 285°

THE CHEAP MATERIAL our sails were cut from continued to be a major flaw in our plan to reach Singapore before the trade winds reversed their flow. This morning I'd emerged from the cabin and encountered more than the usual carnage in our canvas; the jib was flapping in tatters. I was delegated to spend the next few hours, bobbing about on high swells, sewing. Buffeted by winds, tossed by waves; it was a most deranging experience. It was of some small comfort to recall that seventy percent of the Earth's surface is water: this was what 'normal' felt like. *Stability is a luxury for the minority.*

The sea is the largest wilderness of all. The longer you spend on water the closer you come to interpreting its language of deep silence. The more attuned you become to its oceanic whims and tantrums, the keener grows your awareness and appreciation of its myriad reverberations. With growing unease, you realize how little it cares if you perish or survive.

I started writing a letter to Claudia, detailing our voyage so far. I'd earlier washed out an old bottle—its label declared it once housed *Sambal Asli* chili sauce—and had located a suitable cork. This precaution was inspired by the very real suspicion that we were not going to make it. The urge, to not fade into the unknown without leaving behind some tiny piece of us—to have recorded passing this way and justified our actions; to have existed at all—is found within us all. It just takes varying degrees of desperation to unlock.

Claudia my dear,
Wishing you a 'Happy Birthday' for yesterday, though I doubt you'll get this letter by next year since there is no postal service in this neighborhood, eighty miles south of Borneo, in the middle of the Java Sea.

For the past fortnight I've been on an adventure to buy and sail a boat from the far east of Indonesia to Singapore. It's a far cry from when we traveled in that broken down old bus to Lhasa last summer. Already a year!

Along with me are five memorable Frenchmen: Pascal (our egotistical but brave Captain); Xavier, his suave second-in-command (on sabbatical from the Remy Martin Cognac Co.); Gilles (recently fired from his job with the French narcotics agency, having become too involved with his work); Bruno (apparently, a mountaineer of some repute); Franck (whimsical, philosophical, artistic and only twenty— you'd like him). Fredy is from Switzerland (a butchers' son, serious, sensitive and escaping an expired Indonesian visa) ...

To label the Kurnia Ilahi a mere 'boat' is to do her disservice. She's a beautiful, seventy-foot long traditional Bugis perahu, typical of the sloops used for centuries to trade across the seas and up the wide rivers of the Indonesian archipelago. And she's our home. Her hull is made of solid teak wood, and her deck planks, too. She has no engine or metal bolt in her construction. *We rely on the wind for propulsion, a sextant for location, and, should it become necessary, a wooden sampan with a hole in it as our lifeboat for salvation.*

Swells large today, around twelve feet high, they make for a lot of staggering about on deck. We've only been going a week and already have lost the use of our mainsail. We rely for forward motion on our jib; but this, too, has now ripped. We're motionless, at the mercy of the waves. Having drawn the short straw, I've been sent to the prow – the bit that sticks out the front – to reattach the repaired sail. Try threading a needle clinging to the back of an enraged bull, soaring twenty feet above the sea one moment, plunging up to your knees in brine the next. That's what it's like; I'm too scared to even think about being sick.

It's as though I've woken from a dream to find myself wrapped in a nightmare. I can't help but wonder how it all went so wrong, so quickly ... and yet? And yet I'd rather be nowhere else.

I've set aside a bottle with a cork in it, so if we do sink – the possibility is of hourly concern – I can launch this last message to you. By the time you receive it (in a decade or so) you'll know your boy is still an idiot, and still thinking about you ...

Your Chris x

OF CRASHES AND CATERPILLARS

CHARLY AND I had set off on foot: the only sure way of reaching a destination. Early morning sunlight burnt off the fog, revealing snowy spires of megalithic peaks escaping into some incalculable fourth dimension of mass and age. The most suffocating and neck straining of these mountains leaned over, dark and brooding, and proclaimed a primeval independence: "I don't belong to you, you who are just passing through."

At noon we had taken shelter from a chilly downpour in a cattle shed filled to the rafters with carved stones, and religious figurines made out of clay. A dried goatskin had been crucified to the furthest wall, possibly a shamanistic offering to appease older, angrier Gods. The hairs on my neck tingled and I was happy when it stopped raining and we could get moving again.

A newer model *Jiefang* passed us struggling uphill, overladen with massive logs. We outran the truck on the incline, boarding like pirates. Charly did a Spiderman act, swinging from the running board to sit up amongst the timber, and I jumped into the cabin:

"*Tashi Delag!*" — hello! — I tested out my Tibetan on the startled but submissive driver.

Seated in the cab, the brown and green landscape blurring by, I relished the serenity of this, my new life of basics: to find food and water, make shelter for the night, and keep moving forwards. It really was as simple as that. Surely, we'd all be a lot happier paring our lives to these basic parameters, rather than continuously complicating them? All the greed and consumption of the modern world was just a substitute. People bought shit because they were, to varying degrees, unhappy, bored and insecure. News and advertising existed to confirm and increase those fears, desires and feelings of inadequacy. Only by dropping out could we begin to see the truth: how little we need consume to survive. Distractions were the problem. The West was beset by them; swamped by a tidal wave of illusory entertainments, suffocated by endless diversions. Here, there were none. Only the road. Heading ever on to the East.

I turned to look at the driver, to see if he had felt it too, this moment of revelation? But he was twitching, fighting with the wheel, and furiously trying to restart the engine. To conserve fuel, most truck drivers in Tibet coasted their vehicles downhill; it was a reckless economy, but I'd always felt they were in the best position to know their machines and these roads, and it impolite to interject with unwanted advice about health and safety. The *Jiefang* started sluing from one side of the road to the other, an effect exaggerated by its top-heavy load of logs, the physics of which I guessed the driver hadn't taken fully into account when beginning his brake-assisted descent. Charly banged furiously on the roof and shouted something; through the wing mirror I caught a glimpse of his backpack being launched into space, and then Charly following it, in free-fall.

The truck ricocheted off a dirt embankment like a frenzied pinball, slamming into the opposite bank, forcing the door I'd pushed half open to slam back on me. Suddenly everything was inverted. With freeze-frame accuracy I noted the horizon, through the twin eyes of the split windscreen, rotating. One moment my neck was jammed into a corner of the roof, the next I was crashing down on top of the driver. The *Jiefang* screeched and juddered, sliding on its side. It slammed into a deep trench and flipped, finally coming to rest, like a dead cockroach, belly up. A darkness of dust caught up and enveloped us in a storm of stones and pebbles.

"*Ah, merde!*" Charly yanked at the door. The driver moaned, his legs caught by the instrument panel, he was hanging inverted like the sacrificial goat. I kicked at the wedged door with all my remaining strength and, with Charly tugging from outside, it finally came off its hinges allowing me to wiggle out, legs first. Diving back inside the cabin, we freed the suspended driver, aided by the Tibetan goatherd at the foot of who's camp we'd come to such an ignominious rest. The driver smiled like a drunk as we carried him out, in no obvious pain. Then Charly extracted a thermos of *chaang* — the cloudy, beer-like brew made from fermented barley and millet, and found throughout Tibet — from his backpack. With this, he'd set about reviving our spirits.

"It would 'ave been much worse, *mon ami*," Charly smiled in genuine relief, "if my flask, eet 'ad broken."

The beautiful young Tibetan girl, her hair oiled and braided with ornamental lapis, turquoise, and coral, stirred a pan of yak butter tea, bringing it to boil on a wood stove in the center of the tent. Her high cheekbones were accentuated in an angled shaft of sunlight that slashed through the blue smoke; her forehead crinkled in absorption of her task. Gingerly she opened a felt pouch, revealing deep within a few twigs, half a finger long, with a hardened object resembling a dried caterpillar, clinging to each one.

This was the famed Himalayan aphrodisiac, *Cordyceps sinensis*, more commonly known as 'caterpillar fungus', which parasitizes the larvae of the ghost moth, and exists only on the Tibetan Plateau at altitudes exceeding 3,000-meters. The rare medicinal elixir is highly prized in the apothecary markets of Shanghai, Hong Kong and Singapore.

Selecting a single twig, she ground it slowly, deliberately, with pestle and mortar, mixing a few pinches of the resultant powder in tincture with the tea. I assumed it must hold some sort of locally valued remedial properties.

"You think eet is, how you understand, good for men?" Charly's voice was suddenly hoarse with interest.

"You French know better about such things."

"Well, you know, zere are all zose stories. Zese Tibetan women are supposed to be quite independent, huh? It could be like for Gauguin in Ta'iti. Maybe eet is a thing of honor for ze Chief to offer us 'is daughter for ze night?" his eyes glowed, fiery coals of anticipation. "You English, if you do not travel for zis, ze chance encounter, zen why bother to travel at all?"

He had a point. But after a few sips of restorative tea, I blacked out like a light.

THE STORM

Day 8
18:00 hrs: Long. E 111°/Lat. S 4°-Bearing n/a

I WAS JOLTED awake at the tiller by the vigorous rocking of the ship. Having been at sea for a week now, I'd become attuned to the *Kurnia Ilahi*; the way she rolled and recovered after every punch of the waves; the audible tension just before the snapping of a rope; the juddering of her deck planks as she pitched into an oncoming swell. She had become a trusted extension of my body, an integrated part of my central nervous system. But this weather was something new. Something startling.

Franck and I were on the second shift of the night. A vicious lightning storm was raging to starboard, over Borneo, and the temperature had started to drop. A string of lights hugged the horizon—most likely a roaming fishing fleet. The wind was changeable, unpredictable; blowing hard and soft from all directions and making it difficult to steer below 310°. This was bringing us ever closer to the muddy deltas of South Kalimantan, and the hazardous logs Gaby had warned infest these waters.

With the sudden noise of a cracking whip, the rope securing

the jib boom to the mast severed, turning our only sail now into more of a savagely flapping spinnaker, and further depleting the helm of responsiveness. Pascal, awoken for his opinion, said grumpily to leave it until daylight.

At breakfast the decision was made to pull in the jib for repairs, but before we could turn our attention to that task, disaster struck again. This time the cable keeping the entire jib assembly aloft snapped, sending sheet, boom and all, crashing into the drink. We dragged the waterlogged sheet in as fishermen would a fattened trawl net. The winds increased in advance of a sharp squall, rendering any idea of raising the mainsail void. Instead, we reefed the big sheet and carried on drifting.

In the army they say 'never volunteer'. But this was the navy; our lives were closer to the line. Someone needed to go up the mast to help rethread the main line for the jib. Pascal's hand was still bandaged from his time aloft, and Fredy was increasingly pissed off at carrying out all the hard work—this was partly his own fault, of course, needing to prove his bravery in this war of attrition with Pascal—so I stuck my hand up. At least I benefitted from the experience of those who had gone before me. Fredy advised me to wear jeans. The denim felt rough, restrictive and unfamiliar against my now salted and sunburnt legs.

"Here, put this on," Xavier handed me his heavy motorcycle jacket. Thus, protected from splinters and padded against whipping ropes and pulleys, two lifelines were tied around my waist.

"I 'ope so zis one is strong enough." Pascal casually critiqued the fraying fibers of the worst offender. The crew hauled away, the twin ropes creaking as they stretched to take my weight. The ladder, now missing six of its original eighteen rungs was, like a crippled clergyman, able to offer guidance, but no support. Half way up the mast, and the deck already looked tiny. The higher I climbed, the more viciously I was flung through a wide arc, like a pole vault jump looping endlessly on video. The knot of the main life rope dug deep into my solar plexus, making it painful to breathe.

From sixty feet up the ocean appeared an abstract, darkened slate, broken only by advancing ranks of white crested walls, like chalk marks. I triangulated my body; my left foot gripping the uppermost rung of the ladder, my opposite knee bent on the horizontal plank above the jib boom acting as a pincer, and my free arm wrapped around the tip of the mast. I threaded the new rope, praying I'd put it through the correct pulley block. Faith in my crewmates was total, blind: it had to be, or I'd never have risked leaving the safety of the deck. I began the descent, my wet hands struggling to grip the ladder. It was then that we were swamped by a huge wave. Below, I saw Fredy and Bruno being swept across the deck, and the life rope they had been holding going slack, just as the mast tilted over at an alarming angle. I was torn free from the ship, left dangling on the end of a single rope — live bait for some leaping sea monster — the foam roaring now beneath my feet, and unsure if the *Kurnia* would be able to right herself from this surprise assault. Slowly, though, she did, gathering momentum until the mast and rigging began rushing towards me, and I grabbed at an armful of ropes hoping to slow my forward swing. One foot, thankfully, located the ladder.

With our propulsion restored thanks to a working if battered jib, some semblance of stability returned to the deck. Pascal ordered the sacrifice of one of the chickens — the poor birds appeared to have lost any enthusiasm for laying eggs, anyway — hoping perhaps this would appease the weather gods, and diminish the intensity of the gathering storm. The white bird was plumpest.

Fredy, the butcher's son, was handed the captain's machete

and tasked with slaughter. Our resultant feast—the first fresh meat we'd consumed in a week—was grilled, and served with baked potatoes and a homemade garlic sauce. It was stunning testimony to the importance the French place on fine dining, under even the most trying of circumstances.

To the British, nourishment is more an afterthought.

The sea glistened like a silver plate pressed flat by the weight of grey clouds. A little while later there came a strong downpour, and some relief from the vice-like atmospheric pressure. A deeply buried instinct took over us all at the same time, and we rushed to break-out the shampoo and soap. Our own fresh water supply had to be strictly rationed, for cooking with and drinking only. So, we all lathered up on deck. We paid the price for not having bothered to waterproof the cabin roof, though, with leaks spouting all over the place, dampening our bedding.

By early evening we were overtaken by a swift-moving and ominously dark squall, lit from inside by occasional shocks of lightning. The jib flailed in wild indecision, and I was having trouble taming the erratic tiller, the teak arm dragging me across an increasingly slippery deck. Xavier rushed to my side, providing extra manpower and helping to keep the ship turned into the wind. Pascal decided it was time to reef the jib. With no sail left we were at the mercy of the waves. Darkness fell early, and hard. We were almost sitting on the equator, yet it was cold. If we had had a barometer, that smashing sound you just heard was the bottom falling out of it.

"Nobody is allowed to be scared until the captain is scared," shouted Pascal against the howling wind, lightning flashing operatically behind him: "*and I am not scared!*"

We made fast the tiller, tying it into its central position with ropes, so that if we were to drift, our direction would, theoretically, be in a straight line. Any obstruction out there, be it of ship, log or land, was going to have to look out for itself. It being too dangerous to remain on deck, we took refuge in the leaking cabin, sitting in a circle around our sole oil lamp like some fire-worshipping Neanderthal tribe, praying for deliverance.

I'm going to die.

Strangely, now this outcome seemed inevitable and to be arriving at any moment, I discovered I was not so worried. I had travelled too far from home, and experienced an overload of life in the past eighteen months; it was a fair trade-off. Before this point, if I had thought of death at all, it was as something that happened to other people. My optimistic nature, I saw now with blinding clarity, was the product of a lack of imagination: I had been incapable of contemplating an opposite to life. In the past, no matter how serious the situation, I'd always assumed I'd wake to see the sun rise the next day. The world would carry on, with me in it, and the dangers presently being endured would, through the filters of time and perspective, become colorful additions to my growing repertoire of after-dinner tales. But such self-confidence had now deserted me, leaving an unfamiliar void.

One-way tickets should come with a health warning. All I did was set off, trustingly, to Karachi a year-and-a-half ago, and now I was going to perish on the far side of Asia, in the swirling grey sea with a boat full of Frenchmen, dreaming of a big-eyed Bavarian girl who smelt of Tibetan meadows and wood smoke. It all seemed so random.

At least I was not alone in such gloomy assessment of our present chances of survival. Seized by some atavistic communal portend of doom; aware perhaps that there may be no more dinners at which to boast of maritime ordeals, we stuffed ourselves with all the remaining biscuits and luxury food items we could find. It was strange how a full stomach made the prospect of death more palatable. We cracked open our tinned reserves, too. Let's at least go down fully sated. Gilles puffed through all the remaining *kreteks*. I accepted one, too, lung cancer being way down my list of immediate safety concerns.

"We start to worry when we are in the sampan, not before," Pascal's attempt to lighten the mood fell flat. The sampan wasn't tied down: we'd be lucky to get through this tempest without losing our lifeboat over the side. I lost track of how long we rode out the storm, *Kurnia Ilahi* fighting a mighty battle against the crashing waves and swells, her deck scooping up water on each dip.

I wished I'd written to my parents, told them where I was, but that would only have worried them. They'd never find my body out here now. The only chance will be if the message makes it to Claudia in its bottle; she'll tell them of my fate. I tried to envisage how *that* meeting would go. My Mum would exhibit the exemplary politeness of the perfect English hostess, sitting her German visitor down for tea and scones, stoically bracing herself for the delivery of bad news. Decorum would be maintained. Secretly, though, she'd be judging Claudia's discreet ankle tattoo and concluding that this older woman had obviously played some role in steering her boy astray. My Dad would probably fancy her. I made sure the bottle with my letter to her was corked and within reach.

Later. Always later. There can be no precise accounting for chronological time during a storm. Later you'd work it out. Later was good. What was bad was running out of time. Of finding time had ended. That later never arrived. All I had to go on was what my shaken senses were transmitting along the limited number of essential neurological lines of communication my brain kept open. It was freezing, and my teeth wouldn't stop chattering: that much I knew. We huddled together forming a tight circle in the middle of the cabin. To hell with appearances. We hugged each other for warmth and, I guess, some reassurance that since it was just a matter of time before we were shipwrecked, at least we would not be venturing into that vicious, blackened world alone.

I fiddled about trying to fit the cork into the narrow neck of the *Sambal Asli* bottle, now containing my missive to Claudia, but my hands were clumsy and numb. The cabin rotated wildly, attempting to sabotage my efforts. It was as though our ship had been placed inside a giant washing machine; one that had just been switched from rinse cycle to spin. I managed to seal the fragile glass vessel and, grasping hold of a roof beam with one hand as we crested the hissing peak of a gargantuan wave, launched the bottle out the gaping hatchway with all my remaining strength. White salty foam spewed down, filling our sanctuary, dowsing the oil lamp and forcing us all against the farthest wall. We were plunged into darkness, and *Kurnia Ilahi* began her groaning death-plunge into the ocean-hole left behind.

Sometime in the early hours of the morning there came a slight decrease in destructive volatility: the minutest of sea changes, picked up by our strained ears and over-wrought nerves. Franck and I emerged hesitantly from the cabin, thinking we could rescue our shift, but the deck was a scene of utter chaos. In retrospect, it had been a dumb idea to tie-up the tiller. The wooden arm had been split in two struggling to break free from its restraining ropes, like a tree trunk hit by lightning. Fortunately, the rudder itself, connected by the thinnest of umbilical cords — a frayed safety rope — was still dragging behind us, submerged but recoverable. Shards of splintered wood covered the deck; the main boom hung limp, supported only by the shattered remains of the poop deck — our former toilet now offering an empty vista of the sea. Ropes lay scattered around like the forlorn remnants of a wild spaghetti party.

At least we hadn't lost the chickens. They were still alive, swinging from the stern by the string tied to their legs. Come to think of it, Whitey was the lucky one, a swift chop and no having to endure these hours of agonizing water torture. We had lost a further two jerry cans of fresh water, but, on the bright side, there'd been very little disturbance in the hold and we'd taken on surprisingly little additional water below decks.

Yes, the waves were still dangerous; rougher and taller than anything we'd encountered so far: but survival relies on recognizing degrees of improvement, not getting bogged down in absolutes of despair.

A Star for Singapore

Day 9
18:00 hrs: Approx. Long. E 110°/Lat. S 3°–Bearing 320°

THE DOLDRUMS ARE a physical place as well as a state of mind: we had strayed deep into the territory of both. Without wind, the deck was too hot to walk on. We floated along with the current, making at most one knot. I estimated Singapore to be five hundred miles away. On the plus side, three massive oil tankers were visible, steaming westwards on the starboard horizon, following a commercial shipping lane. This suggested the possibility that, if Singapore was their destination, we were at least not too far-off track.

Our clothes, luggage and foodstuffs had been laid to dry on the cabin roof, our offerings to the sun. We busied ourselves scrubbing down the deck, patching up tears and holes in the jib, and organizing any ropes we had left into useable lengths, coiling them in imitation of ordered professionalism.

Pascal took the unilateral decision of lowering the Indonesian flag, raising the Tricoleur in its place. This, he insisted, would change our luck. I thought it extraordinarily lucky for us to have made it this far in the first place. Pascal was contrarily minded, that, were it not for the evil vibes emanating from the red and white ensign, we would already be propped up at the Long Bar in Raffles Hotel, knocking back Singapore Slings.

Indeed, the French contingent were united. They started singing jaunty Breton folk songs and *chants de marins* sea shanties. Further pushing our luck, Gilles began speculating about all the food he'd consume at *Le Meridien* Hotel, upon arrival in the Lion City.

Anglo-Swiss spirits remained somewhat less optimistic.

A quick review of our supplies revealed one pack of biscuits, a box of dried noodles, 20kgs of rice, 3kgs each of potatoes and sugar, two dried fish (the other eight having washed away in the previous night's storm), a few eggplants and fifty coconuts (many of these beginning to go off). Most of the remaining eggs had been smashed. The main problem, apart from Gilles's deteriorating mood now we were out of tobacco, was in having only half-a-pound of coffee left. By some miracle, the dozen bottles of Bintang beer remained unharmed.

The main job of the day was to fix the tiller. We could go nowhere without it. What we *needed* was a drill, some heavy-duty bolts, a welding kit and oxyacetylene torch, and about four square feet of steel plate. What we *had* was a hammer, a small chisel, a hacksaw, a length of wire, and a couple of galvanized nails. After staring down for some moments in contemplation of this pathetic stash, Pascal did what any competent captain would, and dived off the deck, swimming under the keel to check the condition of our semi-detached rudder.

"He's a propeller," muttered Franck, "without any consideration of humanity."

A few hours of smashing, sweating and swearing passed, Pascal and Xavier making a real pig's ear of the tiller. The severed teak arm was bound-up now like a mummy, using all manner of available ropes and wire, and with nails protruding at random angles. I predicted the whole assembly would last a day, maybe two, and that was if conditions remained calm and we were not required to place any unnecessary strain on it. Pascal inhabited a far more buoyant and boisterous mental realm.

"When I get back to France, I will bring *zis* till*air* and put it in my room — with *zis* repair!" our brave capitaine predicted.

And then the wind picked up. The re-patched jib snapped into life, and we began to move forward.

"Look, the wind, she arrives! Quick, where is the video? I must make a film before the jib breaks!"

SOS! Suddenly we were all fully paid-up members of the Singapore Optimist's Society.

Franck

Day 10
18:00 hrs: Approx. Long. E 109°/Lat. S 2°-Bearing 310°

DAWN HAD NOT yet broken; lacking the assurance even of daylight, we were overtaken by a squall that left *Kurnia Ilahi* visiting all points from south to north, the jib unable to decide which side of the ship to favor. Pascal ordered Fredy to man the helm and dragged me out with him onto the prow, or the *balustrade*, as the French picturesquely termed it—one expected flowerpots—where we let out one of the jib ropes, nudging the sail over to starboard. The tiller resented this added responsibility, but remained together in its two pieces.

Utilizing his Jampea kitchen skills, Fredy created a comforting breakfast of sticky rice and desiccated coconut. We chewed on this sweet and filling concoction as a group of around twelve islands—the largest landmass we'd seen since departing the Bugis homeland—drifted in to view. Consulting my map, and Pascal's chart (this was dated 1924, only good for the seas around Singapore, and inscribed with the original Dutch place names), we concluded them to be the Karimata group. Off the northwestern tip of this small archipelago, if the ancient Dutch cartographers were to be believed, flashed a lighthouse. Though I imagine things could have changed in the intervening sixty-four years. If these really were the Karimatas, then we not only had made excellent time, but we were bang on course for Singapore, too.

At 5 p.m., our vessel no more than five miles away from the group, there began a sudden movement, a rippling, like that of a river, as we hit the water channeling in between the two largest islands. We were tugged along by this submerged current,

145

lacking the wind to counter its persuasive flow. It took us on a northerly course of 340° – whereas Singapore lay 350 miles away, on a more westerly bearing – and I prayed the Stowers family 'Curse of Tasman' hadn't chosen this moment to emerge from the woodwork.

As a child, my grandmother used to regale me with stories of her mysterious 'Uncle Tasman', a shadowy descendent she insisted was related to the bumbling Dutch explorer Abel Tasman. Australians would today be calling themselves Tasmanians, had distant ancestor Abel not missed an entire continent on his way to discovering a wild, beautiful, but ultimately less than world-shattering island, slightly further to its south.

This evening's comic relief was provided, after dinner, when Xavier, having washed-up the dishes in a bucket, inadvertently launched most of our cutlery overboard in a silvery cascade, along with the soapy water.

Since the loss of our toilet to storm damage on the poop deck, we'd relocated the loo to the prow where balanced carefully, with a foot on either of the two minor anchors, one swayed and plunged in privacy over a soothing rush of sea. It was as I squatted thus, contemplating the finale of a most spectacular sunset, the heavily forested slopes of the Karimata group merging into solid hue, that I became distracted by excited shouting from the helm. We were passing the northern tip of Serutu island and, bang on cue, there was the signal from the lighthouse shown on Pascal's ancient map: three flashes in succession and then a gap of five seconds. Freed from the conveyor belt of the mid-island channel, and picking up a stiff breeze off of Kalimantan – now behind us – we were able to maneuver to the more westerly bearing of 290°.

The Singapore Star appeared directly ahead.

CELESTIAL NAVIGATION

THERE ARE SO many stars. Popular mythology has it we are all constituted of their dust. I've always been skeptical of that saccharine and rather Hallmark sentiment. Yet somehow, when you find yourself alone and floating in the middle of a vast black ocean, with no visible horizon or earthly point of reference, it is impossible not to gaze towards the astral vault and become absorbed in its infinite detail and precision. Like a compass needle, being tugged to north by the faintest resonance of magnetic matter, so we who came from the stars turn our heads irresistibly towards them. The possibility begs to be considered that what we are dreaming of as yielding to these celestial urgings—what we are yearning for—is to find our way back home.

The last time I'd found myself this close to the Heavens was when crossing Tibet, with Charly. There, the total lack of pollution and high, airless, altitude rewarded us with phenomenal clarity. At the time we had Polaris, the North Star, to provide some stability in a roving and nomadic sky. It was fascinating to observe and calculate where the different constellations lay in relationship to each other—and perhaps all those meds on an empty stomach had been kicking-in, too. It was all very Van Gogh. We hadn't needed to *rely* on the stars, though, since we had the road; and that was simply going either west back to Lhasa, or east on to Chengdu.

Now I was in the Southern Hemisphere, and Polaris no longer a reliable guide. Pascal had taken over the astrological lessons and taught me how to calculate Due South by using the Southern Cross. This close to the equator the cluster sat just above the horizon. What you did was extend a line along its main axis for a distance of about 4.5 times that of the gap between the top and bottom stars of the cross. Next, you locate the two bright stars above it, The Pointers, and draw a line perpendicular through these. Where the two lines intersect will be directly above South.

As long as I kept 'south' slightly behind my left shoulder when I was at the tiller, then we'd be heading at our preferred vector of around 280°, give or take some tugging of the currents and tumbling on the waves.

CROSSING THE EQUATOR
(WITH FOOD AFORETHOUGHT)

Day 11
18:00 hrs: Approx. Long. E 108°/Lat. S 1°-Bearing 300°

FREDY AND I emerged bleary-eyed from the cabin and took over the night shift from Franck and Gilles. Pascal had been up, too — he *never* seemed to sleep — and left us a communal bowl of the rice pudding mixed with brown sugar and cinnamon he'd concocted. We had to scoop the food with our hands now, thanks to Xavier's casual dispersal of our silverware the day before. Dolphins again accompanied us, and I began to question my earlier assumption, that they were all just showing off. Perhaps they saw in our ungainly hull a wounded fellow sea mammal, and swam around us offering protection? Certainly, I always felt my stress levels decrease when these placid and playful creatures were around, swooping and leaping alongside and beneath the *Kurnia Ilahi*, like the very current itself.

At one point the wind caught the main boom, tightening a rope attached to it which leapt up, ripping the scab off my left

shin. That wound had been healing nicely since being savaged
by the deck early on in the voyage; back in the days of innocence
when I'd thought that that was the worst that could go wrong.
My feet were still cut up, and chest bruised, from my excursion
up the mast, too. I guessed I'd survive, and was putting all my
faith in the antiseptic qualities of a twice-daily salt-water shower
(or *mandi*, the local term we'd adopted, way back in Maumere).

"More knots than an Englishman's handkerchief, *non?*" Pascal
boasted with pride. We were staring up at the tangled mess of the
jib and its confusion of ropes. But he meant our speed. This was
a surprisingly rapid five knots. It was pushing things, just as he
liked to: we'd long established *Kurnia's* comfort zone was a more
sedate 3-4 knots. The patched sail was straining at its supporting
wire, held on by only twelve of its original twenty-four metal
rings, and new tears kept appearing all the time.

"Yes," I replied, "and more holes than your underpants." He
hadn't worn anything else since leaving Jampea. He just grinned.

At noon our captain continued with his stubborn tradition
of taking a reading with the sextant. Supertramp's *Breakfast in
America* album played over the speakers. The sea had turned
deep blue, a pleasant change from the earlier murky greens and
muddy browns, diluted with the sedimentary run-off of Borneo.
A Chinese-registered container ship, riding fast and empty,
ploughed through the waves, forcing an impressive plume at
her bow. From her bridge the crew looked down on us, and I felt
immense pride at being a part of this piratical venture.

Day 12
18:00 hrs: Approx. Long. E 107°/0°–Bearing 295°

I HAVE CROSSED the equator by air: it was unremarkable. We live in an age accustomed to miracles, our sense of wonder neutered by the ease and availability of long-distance travel. We fly above the territory brave adventurers gave their lives to map, and consider a three-hour stopover in the transit lounge an unpardonable inconvenience. How soft and spoilt we have become. By sea, on a sailboat, at least, some sense of proportion and tradition remain.

There was no thin red ribbon running around the sweaty waistband of the world, no welcoming canoe with natives offering souvenir '*I Survived 0°*' T-shirts—though that's a commercial opportunity begging to be exploited. The waters failed to boil and foam with mysterious sea creatures. I imagine, as with most profound discoveries, the equator was stumbled upon by accident, the stars stubbornly refusing to compute: new constellations arising, along with the possibility of virgin lands to explore. Quite possibly there would have been some relief at not having fallen off the edge of the world, too.

We had lost two more rings from the jib line in the night. Our only functioning sail was now held in place by ten small metal circlets. It was going to be a race to get to Singapore before they gave out completely. Tropical weather is schizophrenic: from sun to storm with no warning of mood change. Two separate squalls converged, signaling their arrival by angrily twanging the jib pulley and promptly sending the sail plummeting into the sea. We reacted to this now commonplace occurrence with consummate professionalism, dragging the dripping sheet back on board. Then, with memories of the big storm a few days ago resurfacing, we retreated to the cabin to sit the tempest out. I picked unenthusiastically at one of Pascal's least edible creations to date, *risotto au sel de la mer* — as advertised: rice, boiled in sea water.

Sliding around inside the damp cabin, caught in a crashing tangle of luggage and unlashed food supplies, I rued my lack of dedication back on Jampea to load the hold with just two, rather than a more appropriate twenty, tons of sand. A *perahu* like *Kurnia Ilahi* is designed to sit fat and low in the water, letting waves roll over her. Instead, she rode impressively high. And whilst this was esthetically pleasing, it led to a lot of impractical — and potentially disastrous — rolling around. But I was not mortally scared now: *Kurnia's* flawed accessories of sail, pulley and rope may have been weak, but these were replaceable. Her tropical teak heart — the hull — was strong.

Still, a fine line existed between confidence and a nonchalant disregard for life and limb. It was a line Pascal had chewed up and spat out long before this voyage. No sooner had we lowered him back from fixing the main jib pulley, than he carelessly tossed a valuable length of rope to Xavier. It was caught in the wind and sent uncoiling into the sea, where it started to sink beneath the boat. Pausing only to order Franck to drop a ladder over the port side, he dived in after the rope. We had long ago re-employed the stern safety line to haul up the mainsail, so Fredy and I, acting on impulse, grabbed the longest bamboo pole from the hold, and pushed it off the splintered remains of the poop deck, as far as it would go. At length, Pascal resurfaced, the end of the rescued rope gritted between his teeth. He lunged at the bamboo pole and we hauled him around to the ladder. There was no way we could have turned the boat back for him had he missed the pole.

Perhaps intent on calmly enjoying the show along with us, the wind dropped its act in time for sunset. We had been dragging our dozen bottles of precious Bintang beer in the sea all day to cool them down, but the liquid was still warm. Pascal ordered us all to attention and then paused for the sake of drama — at least he didn't start to sing *Le Marseilles* — and for Franck to fiddle with the video controls, before pronouncing us *back in the Northern Hemisphere!* We cracked open the bottles; after a month with no alcohol, the bubbles shot straight to my head, and the booze numbed the extremities of my limbs.

I located a patch of warm deck to lie on and imagined Claudia was there beside me — I could think of no other I would like to share this memory with — and stared up in wonder through the knotted mass of rigging at the myriad stars, mesmerized by the swish of the hull. *Kurnia Ilahi* slipped through gently swelling waves, and I wished to remain suspended forever in this blissful void.

What had Chekov written about moments like this? *"Don't run away from your happiness. Take it while it offers itself to you freely, later you will be running after it, but you won't overtake it."*

That sounded about right.

Day 13
18:00 hrs: Approx. Long. E 106°/Lat. N 1°–Bearing 280°

AT 4 A.M. BRUNO awoke me with a shrill whistle from the helm. I'd fallen asleep on watch. We had to be on our guard for small boats, and for signs of land on our approach to the Indonesian islands south of Singapore. An increase in fishing floats and beacons, and sighting of small birds; these were the usual giveaways.

"Do you see that?" he said, pointing almost directly ahead, at 300°. "It could be a forest fire, do you think?"

What he had spotted was a semi-circular glow on the horizon. Not a direct light — so that counted out any fishing fleet — but one that was not getting any larger, either, no matter how long we held our course towards it.

"It has to be Singapore!" I exclaimed suddenly and without a shadow of doubt, remembering the glow I grew up with, viewed from the high point in the fields opposite my home; the luminescent aura emanating from the distant financial district of London.

Following my shift, I remained on deck. My spine was by this time covered in sores, the result of constantly banging it on the low cabin ceiling, so I preferred to laze at the base of the mast. Idly twiddling the dials on Xavier's AM radio, a voice in English broke through the static, making me jump. I moved the radio around to where the signal was strongest — about 290/300° — and SBC, the Singapore Broadcasting Corporation, came through with the first news from the outside world in over a month:

The Olympics in Seoul had just started and the USSR was ahead with 16 medals to the USA's 5. The Woman's Marathon had been won by Portugal (in 2nd place, Australia, and picking up the Bronze, East Germany). There had been landslides in Nepal, and the United States was withdrawing aid from Burma ...

I imagined I could do without news for another month.

The French were becoming unbearable as our food rations diminished. They decided, unilaterally, that the remaining chickens were for the pot tonight. But Fredy refused to kill again. And still repairs needed to be made to the jib. Pascal let us do all the work today, standing around, laughing at our efforts to contain the sail in a strong wind, only condescending to lend a hand when he'd had enough of the game and wanted to get a move on. He could be a real bastard, at times. But he *could* cook.

When, in late 1789, French physician Joseph-Ignace Guillotin first proposed the use of a special device to carry out executions in a more humane manner, and in accordance with new Enlightenment ideals about human rights, he neglected to add a clause ensuring the swift dispatch, by this method, of chickens. Zooming forward almost two hundred years, we arrive at the deck of the not-quite-so progressively-minded French-Bugis ship *Kurnia Ilahi*, bobbing in placid waters somewhere off the west coast of tropical Borneo, just north of the equator.

As big Gilles held down the vaguely resisting body of our last scrawny bird, Franck stepped up to the plate, armed with the hacksaw. Pulling the hen's neck thin, he speculated aloud:

"This should make a nice *sanglette*," and he placed a bowl on the deck to contain the expected outpouring of warm blood. The life fluid of a fowl, when mixed with an appropriate concoction of onions, garlic and spices, he assured me, would transform into a tasty version of the traditional sticky sauce favoured by farmers in some of the more remote regions of the French interior.

"We don't eat it these days," Franck dismissed, "but since we have the opportunity ..." he strained, hacking at sinew with the blunt blade, "... it would be a pity not to try."

Slaughter took some time, Pascal avidly filming the entire gruesome spectacle on video, relishing the opportunity to sever heads. I hid away in the cabin, unable to watch, emerging only after the deed had been done. Then Pascal handed the deflated hen to Fredy for him to pluck. Our victorious evening meal, of diced chicken, fried with the last remaining packets of instant noodles, and garlic — with its dubious glazing of hen's blood — was washed down with three bottles of flat beer left over from last night's party. The Jampea well water in the big barrel, tasting rather brackish by now, was safe to drink only when boiled.

Momentarily sated, and thinking 'well, that's all our food gone now, so we *have* to arrive in Singapore soon', I went to rest my back against the mast. I think I must have fallen asleep, as I started to dream about the previous year, when Charly and I had arrived in Dege, a mountainous town at the natural boundary between Tibet and China. We'd immediately celebrated this milestone by ordering up a feast; something we'd been only able to dream of doing during the past thousand kilometers. Almost a thousand more still lay before us, to Chengdu, but the mere act of crossing the upper reaches of the youthful Yangtze River here had reignited hope.

And where there is hope, soon follows appetite.

At first glance, Dege was an affluent Tibetan settlement. Solid, single-storey flat roofed stone buildings, painted in white and maroon, were stacked like boxes up both sides of its steep valley. The towns' cracked cement paths were traversed by farmers perched on slow-chugging rotary tillers, a few people on bicycles, and by wild-faced, longhaired herdsmen, on horseback.

Four of Asia's mightiest rivers — the Mekong, Yangtze, Yellow and Salween — spring to life in the mountains and snowfields of Dege's Kham region. And high above the town, in a courtyard behind a newly constructed small shrine, or *gompa*, sat Parkhang Monastery, a priceless repository of thousands of Buddhist scriptures and wooden printing blocks that had somehow survived the ravages of the Cultural Revolution. Here, an army of devoted monks and craftsmen bent over low tables in gloomy, candle-lit rooms, furiously carving new tablets. Others sat in pairs, using rollers to apply cotton and paper across surfaces coated with ink to produce new prayer flags and pages of sacred text.

As with all border towns, Dege — which, since the 10th century, had never yielded to the authority of Lhasa for any extended period of time, and only came under direct Chinese authority, grudgingly, after the communist takeover in the 1950s — was leading a double life: comfortably embracing the qualities of both its contemporary halves, swearing allegiance to neither. It offered a first glimpse at the modern Chinese world of commerce, electricity and concrete, yet remained a stubborn holdout of nomadic tradition.

But a nomad has to eat, and greasy, uncooked barley flour could sustain the wandering stomach only for so long. Charly and I devoured greedily a many-plated meal at a Chinese-run restaurant. Pork and chicken, fried onions and tomatoes, cabbage laced with garlic slices and mushrooms, all drowned by ladles full of splendiferous sauces. My neglected and withered taste receptors, punished by weeks consuming only *tsampa* and yak fat, didn't quite know what to make of the sudden reintroduction of garlic, star anise and chili peppers to the palate, to say nothing of the discovery of Sichuan Peppercorns. The intense, citrus-like tanginess of these combined with a dynamite, mouth numbing kick, at once definitive yet not overpowering of the other ingredients in any dish. We polished off three bowls of rice each, and several bottles of beer. Total cost: 5RMB (less than a dollar). Chinese culture, we felt certain at the time, was most successfully being asserted through the magic of the wok, rather than the barrel of a gun.

I awoke on the hard deck on a rolling sea, my stomach rumbling, and secretly glad we would not make it to Singapore tonight. Attempting to navigate through a harbor live with supertankers, in the dark, and without the aid of an engine or any proper lights, was foolhardy. But so was setting off from Jampea in the first place.

One concern nagged at me: if Singapore was so close, how come we'd not sighted any of the Riau group of islands that ought to litter its approach? Had we perhaps been over-compensating, keeping too long on the 300° heading? Were we, instead, being pulled north by some invisible tide? What if we had overshot Singapore already? If that were the case, we'd have to head directly west and beach *Kurnia Ilahi* on the Malaysian shoreline. For once I was glad of Pascal's self-assured optimism:

"We keep going on 290°. Why do you want to see any islands? Better is to avoid them, no?"

A SAFETY BRIEFING

THOUGH ALL OF us were dog-tired, none of us could sleep: arrival was in the air. Singapore, like 'tomorrow', lay over the horizon, just out of reach. Our noon sextant reading was of no use, calculating a range of possibilities between 2-10° North, which was impossible ... surely? Singapore is positioned slightly above the equator, at around Latitude N 1.3°. My readings, if accurate, would have *Kurnia Ilahi* drifting far to the north of the Lion City. We were getting through a gallon-a-day each of fresh water, and needed to land *somewhere* soon. Pascal was more edgy than usual, wanting to use the mainsail. But this had only ever brought us bad luck, and the rest of us out-voted him.

Mid-afternoon, glistening mirage time. Was that land I just spotted? Distant and hazy, but most definitely Ho! "Land, land, over there (*what the hell is the French word for land?*)!" Only, whose? The Indonesians? Malaysians? Luckily a small, motorized launch with Indonesian markings was heading straight toward us, *the Coast Guard?* Battling stoically through adverse waves, it heaved to, alongside. We were relieved it contained a smiling face, and no uniform. Securing our boats with ropes fore and aft, the fisherman jumped aboard. Fredy tried to extract our current position, but even our Swiss linguist couldn't make out what the little Indonesian was saying. For his part, the captain of the launch seemed more interested in Xavier's binoculars than our questions. Gilles was the first to make a breakthrough, using universal sign language to mime his desperation for a cigarette. The Indonesian hopped back to his launch, disappearing inside its cabin; Pascal signaled that we should get the machetes out, just to be safe. The fisherman returned with a carton of Gudang Garams and Pascal distracted him with the map.

Now, in certain countries and cultures outcomes are most effectively and speedily achieved through straight talk, and the occasional strategic loss of temper. In Indonesia, employment of these exact same methods first renders the accosted individual in a state of slavish solicitude. If insisted upon, they ignite a toxic environment of non-cooperation and, at some unexpected future moment, lead to you being stabbed down a dark alleyway. Pascal was losing his temper, a state of affairs the rest of us had become used to, and took with a pinch of abundant sea salt. But his mannerisms were making the Indonesian jittery. Finally, the harassed fisherman pointed to a port on the map, cast a wary eye around the seven armed and disheveled foreign devils closing in, judged it wise to drop his quest for the binoculars, and legged it back to his boat. He didn't even wait for us to pay for the *kreteks*.

"Tanjung Pinang!" exulted Fredy, all business. "I'm guessing that's his home port. So, we're looking at Bintan island, or at least the small islands just southeast of it." If we were to keep at a heading of 300° for sixty miles, we should pass the lighthouse on its northernmost tip. "And that, my friends, is the entrance to the Singapore Strait."

It was 4 p.m., and a safety briefing from Pascal — the emphasis being on 'brief' — as we were sucked into the vortex of Singapore Harbor:

"If we are pulled in under a supertank*air* because of no wind, do not push off with your feet: it is easy to lose your leg ... just wait and see, *huh*?"

And that was it. It appeared we had no option but to drift across one of the world's busiest commercial shipping routes undercover of the night.

"It was always going to end like this," muttered Franck, darkly. Gilles handed me four new Duracell batteries, for my torch, for emergency signaling. Heavy granite skies threatened rain over the islands to port. They filled me with dread, and obscured our final sunset. As blackness descended, I counted thirteen container ships and oil tankers around us, on all sides, and prayed their night watchmen had eaten an extra ration of carrots. We cleared the decks for action; checked that what was left of the rigging moved smoothly through the pulleys, and topped up the oil lamp using the last of the paraffin. At 7 p.m., we spotted Bintan island's huge northern lighthouse, dead ahead, pulsing out one flash every ten seconds, and marking the entrance to the South Channel.

By 8 p.m. we were approximately eight miles due east of the lighthouse. In order to round the cape and tack to follow the channel west (on a course of 240-270°) we'd have to raise the mainsail, or the current would drag us too far north, towards Peninsula Malaysia. All the lights of all the boats on the ocean seemed to be converging on this lighthouse from every point of the compass. It was a magical, daunting sight.

9 p.m.: The jib was clinging on now by just its top and bottom rings. It was no longer possible to avoid the inevitable.

"*La grand-voile!*" shouted Pascal. "Pull her up, the mainsail."

An almost full moon eased our task, it being the Chinese Mid-Autumn Festival this weekend. An auspicious date to attempt arrival. On the second try we got our ropes in the correct order and the sail billowed outwards, a silvery beacon in the moonlight. Bruno, on the tiller, sounded surprised: "It is working! We are coming around."

At this pronouncement, we all came alive, whistling and cheering as tying-off the ropes. A thankful *Kurnia Ilahi*, intent on showing us what she was made of, turned easily to a course of 210°. This was closer to 230°, when corrected for the current.

For the next two hours, we traced the northern coast of Bintan island, trying to keep a safe distance from the major shipping lanes and anchorages, whilst avoiding entanglement with the shrimp platforms dotting its shallows. I had control of the tiller for an hour, and Xavier took over at 11 p.m., pulling us up to around 260°. Probably I should have tried to get some sleep; it'd be all hands on deck when we cut across to Singapore island … and yet, the night was so dreamlike, I was probably asleep already. I found myself on the roof of the cabin, listening to Pascal who was planning his next sailing adventure.

"I will buy a 100-foot schooner from Bonerate and sail via Hawaii to San Diego. There I will sell it for a fortune. This time we will have proper ropes and a proper sail. I will write to you and you must join us!" I *must* have been dreaming for I heard myself say "Yes".

Midnight. Sail and moonlight. I stood alone at the bow, draped in gossamer translucence: my shadow a stain on the warped deck behind. We'd changed course: north-by-northwest. Pascal was gambling that Changi was situated above us. We would just have to cut through the shipping lanes of both the South and Middle Channels to reach it.

"Chris, you get to the front with the lamp, swing it at anything that moves!"

To the photographer, the sun is a reliable wife. With her, I work in
partnership creating images; I admire her rising calm and setting
beauty, and toil under the ferocity of her knowing stare. The sun
lights my life and shows me the way. The moon, on the other
hand, is a capricious mistress. I am reborn and caressed by her
ephemeral shimmer, and hide my fears in her darkest recess. The
moon ignites my desires and always leads me astray. The one is
but the reflection of the other.

I stared absently ahead, into the space where moon and stars
should be. Only tonight, it seemed, they had been cleared like
bugs off a screen. I could hear the whooshing of the celestial
wiper, getting louder, erasing more stars. And then moonlight
glinted off an advancing valley of waves, parting like the Red
Sea before Moses. The rushing of the water was accompanied
by a deafening mechanical throb, and, rising from the vacuum
of darkness, a ten-storey supertanker came right at us. The ship
must have been a quarter mile in length; it was a city afloat. I
started frantically swinging the oil lamp from side to side and
flashing my torch in the direction of an invisible bridge, but it
was of no use. Our wooden vessel would not show up on their
radar, and they wouldn't be able to alter course, even if they did
spot us.

"Jesus," I gasped, lungs in my throat. "Attention ... *Attention!*"
Gilles and Franck were beside me in a flash, both readying
poles; Pascal joined Xavier on the tiller, together they pushed
the fragile arm to stern, managing to squeeze us a few degrees
further north, but at a loss of tension in the sheet. It was merely
a matter of luck now: direct hit or glancing blow. Ought we
vainly attempt to save *Kurnia* by rushing to her port side and
fending off this charging steel monster with our pathetic arsenal

of bamboo sticks? Or jump for it, like ungrateful cowards? There was no time. The specter of certain doom rarely exposes itself to lingering inspection.

An artificial tsunami was being created by the supertanker's ploughed tide. Lifted by a colossal liquid hand, *Kurnia Ilahi* rose, shuddering and groaning deep from within her hull, a primal release of resentment that shook itself out at the very tip of her mast.

Bruno and Franck dropped their spikes in the rush to grab a hold of any solid section of soaring deck and cabin. Pascal grimly wrapped himself around the tiller and I hugged the prow, riding the neck of this seabird as she attempted lift-off. Up and up we surged until, finally, breaking and tilting to starboard, we swooped down across the busy sea roads, a scudding moonlit ghost ship, mainsail straining to contain the tempestuous forces pushed before a rushing wall of steel ...

PART

4

SINGAPORE!

FOLLOWING OUR NEAR miss in the South Channel, I must have fallen asleep, deprived of the energy to care whether we made it or not. Next thing I knew it was 4 a.m. and Fredy was shaking me awake, shoving a ridiculously sweet cup of tea under my nose: "Here, drink this and come on deck. We have a problem." *Is this night ever going to end?*

The trouble this time stemmed from Pascal's antiquated chart of Singapore, the City State's various ports and shipping channels, land reclamations and innovations, such as the International Airport at Changi, having altered considerably since the 1920s. It had been this, the semispherical glow from Changi Airport's floodlit runway—now blinding our approach—that Bruno had spotted two nights before. Ignoring the fact that regional cargo vessels were officially required to dock in the Barter Trade Zone at Pasir Panjang (now a huge and modern container port) on Singapore's southern shore, Pascal instead insisted we head for a berth at Changi Sailing Club, reserve of champagne-sipping expats, eastwards up the Johor Strait.

Inveterate sea-traders, the Bugis have historically enjoyed a profitable association with Singapore. As such, I was sure we were not the first Bugis vessel or crew to have faced the dilemma of where to dock. The annual arrival of their 'mosquito fleet' on the September-October trade winds was a spectacle eagerly anticipated by shopkeepers and consumers in the former British Colony. And many a Bugis captain must have been tempted to sail straight into Marina Bay and start selling directly from his deck to a public anxious to get their hands on the exotic goods carried in his hold. Particularly desired were the Bird of Paradise feathers, bird's nests, beeswax and gold dust, tortoise shell, sandalwood, mother-of-pearl and *Sarong Bugis* (as their durable woven fabric was known) that, along with cotton and coffee, were imported on ships almost identical to *Kurnia Ilahi* for centuries. Until the late 1960s, fleets of up to 250 *perahu* would dock in the Kallang River and at Sandy Point, close to the location of Bugis Street, today. The Barter Trade Zone was created in the 1970s to better regulate the flow of trade and traffic in an increasingly hectic harbor. 'Regulation' being a concept if not completely unknown, then at least distasteful to the Bugis, by the mid-1970s around only twenty *perahu* were making the annual pilgrimage (and, with the closure of the Pasir Panjang facility in 1995 officially consigning the annual spectacle of the 'mosquito fleet' to a footnote of Singapore's maritime history, *Kurnia Ilahi* was almost certainly one of the last traditional, un-motorized *perahu* to ever make the voyage).

The decision as to our own arrival venue was both stark and fast approaching. The entrance to the Johor Strait, east of Singapore, should have been visible, but nothing so identifiable presented itself. The chart was useless. We were going to have to rely on some pretty smart Bugis guesswork, instead. With no engine to help us counter the whims of Nature, we were keenly aware that if we missed the channel on this first attempt, we'd not be able to go against the current for a second try. I strained my eyes, taking in the shadowy landmass — was it a cape? — that inhibited our direct approach. It could be Singapore's Tekong island. Or the tip of mainland Malaysia. Changi's bright lights attracted us like moths to a flame, dead ahead, but by following them blindly we risked losing the ability to tack sharply enough to enter the Johor Strait, should that option suddenly appear.

"So, we take a vote," Pascal resorted to uncharacteristic democracy. This time I found myself with the winning majority who decided carrying on to the observable reality of Changi, preferable to veering into the gulping void. Just before the sun broke above the mangroves, absorbing all artificial light, Gilles spotted a bobbing red beacon. This signaled the eastern entrance to the Johor Strait. An exhausted wisp of wind allowed us to tack starboard using the mainsail, and avoid being swept to shipwreck on Changi Point. At the final meander masts swayed visibly above Changi Village, like extensions to the trees, pinpointing our objective. And then the breeze deserted us. We drifted along on the flow. Commuter ferries crowded with white-shirted office workers crossed our path, coming in from *Pulau Ubin* and Johor. In accordance with the ancient maritime precedence given sail over motor, these altered course around us.

I took this moment to observe my sun-browned crewmates: Gilles, a *kretek* angled in the corner of his mouth, wincing against pungent clove fumes; Bruno, as thin as a bamboo pole, leaning back on a rope, keeping the mainsail aloft by willpower alone; Fredy, standing atop the cabin, lost in a dream, perhaps already tired of this adventure, picking up scent of his next. Emergency had advanced our education. Two weeks ago, none of us knew one end of a rope from the other. Now I could thread a pulley block at the top of a swaying mast in a storm, and steer a boat with some confidence using only the stars for guidance. We put on a show in front of the gawping ferry passengers, collapsing our mainsail with theatrical flair. I hoped this intrusion into their daily routine would give them something to dream about as they headed on to their jobs in the City. One or two ventured to wave at us and we responded ecstatically, high after our sleepless night of taut nerves and drama. High at having arrived here at all; common sense screaming we should be dead by now.

Having come this far, we now couldn't stop. Slowly we drifted past the whitewashed building of Changi Sailing Club. A tugboat was refueling at the floating Shell station in mid-channel. Pascal hailed its crew and they quickly assessed our dilemma. Franck and I hastened to the fore and untied one of the minor anchor ropes there. This we tossed down to the tug when it chugged beneath our bow to use as a tow line. For a final ten-minutes, after fully two-weeks at sea, we acquiesced to motorized assistance. The tugboat pulled our Bugis pirate ship against the current to moor on the outer perimeter of all the fancy yachts.

The German owner of the boat closest to us — the *Aphrodite* — dispatched his Filipino crewman in a motor-dinghy to our aid, helping us reposition the second anchor. A colorful assortment of ropes, all of odd lengths and in varying states of repair, needed now to be hastily tied together if there was any chance of it reaching the estuary mud.

It was 3 p.m., and the afternoon rains gathered for their daily assault. We had managed to re-patch the hole in the sampan, using for this purpose half a pack of chewed gum. Fredy returned from having ferried Pascal, Gilles and Franck to shore, reporting the bodge-job repair a success. I shot the last frame of my final roll of Ektachrome; a picture of Fredy paddling towards us, dark clouds amassing, and the sailing club's main structure shining brilliant in its reflective white paint, on the distant shore. Two rolls of film: an adventure told in seventy-two images. I hoped something would come of it, though realistically, I had been too busy trying to keep the ship afloat most of the time to worry about my photographic duties. Lowering our luggage to Fredy, I stepped gingerly aboard the oscillating canoe. Bruno, Xavier and their bags followed, bringing us perilously close to the water. At first the going was easy, but then the heavens opened. On cue, the chewing gum popped out of its hole, chased by a fountain of seawater. I signaled desperately to the German captain of *Aphrodite* who again kindly dispatched his Filipino crewman. Our backpacks safely transferred to his rubber dinghy, Fredy doggedly continued to paddle, our progress now the focus of a mob of club members who were massing on the second-floor verandah. A gargantuan Japanese container ship chose this moment to motor through the channel. Waves three-feet-high fanned out in her wake. We saw them coming and yet were powerless to stop them: water swamped us on all fronts; washing over the sides, jetting-in through the hull, and still pouring from the skies. The sampan, our much-maligned but until now faithful ferry, surrendered and sank. We entered Singapore, wading out of the Johor Strait, tugging our submerged lifeboat by its painter and greeted by the cheers, whistling and sarcastic comments of the gin-soaked spectators above. I felt like kissing the sand: *we have arrived!* But that would have just encouraged them.

Securing the sampan beneath the jetty, we headed to the shower room to indulge, for me at least, in the first encounter with hot, fresh water since Darwin. Spruced-up, we next hit the sailing club restaurant, devouring sausages, baked beans, egg and chips with garlic bread, all washed down with chilled beer. Extra chips, obviously, followed by coffee, ice cream and more beers for dessert. Gilles smoked a Cuban cigar, and we left him in deep discussion with the bartender. Later in the evening, we all automatically headed back out to *Kurnia Ilahi*. The idea of finding a hotel in the city didn't enter my mind. We'd all become used to lying on the worn planks of her cabin, and tonight I knew I'd sleep aboard our beautiful Bugis ship free of charge, untroubled by the need to keep watch or worry about sinking.

At around 3 a.m. I was awoken by the sound of excited giggling on deck, and Gilles slurring his words, drunk. I poked my head through the shaded door hatch. Gilles was leaning back on the bow rails, staring up at the stars through closed eyes. Surrounding him were three glamorous, leggy women, as easy on the eye as — it would appear — of virtue. I decided not to intervene as he had the situation under control.

172

ARRIVALS AND DEPARTURES

CHARLY AND I had crossed the Yangtze (known in this section as the Minjiang) River again, twenty miles out of the Sichuan provincial capital, Chengdu. The river was much wider here than at Dege, and flowed slower. Exhausted of youthful exuberance — accepting of the smoother, shallower boundaries it had to travel between, rather than fighting them — it seemed to have made the inevitable trade-off guaranteeing longevity and power, and the long haul to the sea.

The end of the road was the courtyard of a huge hotel complex near Chengdu's long distance bus station. Now we'd actually arrived, I couldn't bring myself to descend from the cabin of the truck. Why are we always in such a rush to get to a destination, only to leave it again, to cast it aside? It was a betrayal of the spirit of a month that, an instant ago, had seemed so vital and permanent. The pain, the cold and hunger, these I had already forgotten. And in their place was a sense of loss, a faint ache in the gut.

I longed only to run wild and free on Tibetan roads again.

Charly, ever practical, soon located a cheap and serviceable room in an annex behind the hotel. It had a black and white TV upon which International Students' Athletics from Yugoslavia were being aired. And then he suggested heading out to fulfill our search for coffee. The combination of several sachets of *Maxwell House* instant granules, dissolved in sweet condensed milk, acted like a blood transfusion to my serried veins.

Solitude was not hard to come by in this city of several million people. I felt displaced and ignored, more isolated than when tramping the most desolate steppe. I handed ten *fen* to a street urchin and weighed myself on his set of scales. I'd lost just over a stone (equivalent to 14lbs, for any American readers, or somewhere around 7kgs, for those more familiar with the metric system) in the twenty-five days since setting out from Lhasa.

Later that evening Charly arrived back from the city's main railway station, excited and waving his onward ticket to Kunming. My sole living connection to Claudia would be soon moving away, and he looked pretty happy to be getting back on his own again too, without me to slow him down any longer.

"Hurry, Chris. Ze bathhouse will close soon."

I imagined Turkish steam baths were somewhat similar. The communal heated pool. The wooden pigeon holes in which to store clothes and valuables. I sat naked, sweating on the concrete rim alongside an aged Chinaman, one of whose testicles was swollen to half the size of a football. I was thinking twice about sinking into the warm, cloudy waters beside him. Very likely he harbored similar doubts about sharing the water with a pair of long-nosed, foreign devils, too.

Following a long steaming, and feeling suddenly quite faint, I staggered over to an adjacent row of shower nozzles. I allowed my body to be blasted with cold water, and washed my hair, relishing the luxury of shampoo and soap for the first time in a month.

"Your leg, *mon ami*, look at eet!"

Oh God, what now? My stomach recoiled. The harsh jet of water had dissolved the layer of mud encrusting my ankles, leaving them exposed, red and raw. And then? Nothing. No swelling, no pus, no more pain. "Eet 'as to be zose caterpillars!" Charly was convinced of it.

The next time Fate arranged for Charly and I to meet was on the narrow staircase leading up to *Lucky Guesthouse,* in Kowloon. Four months had passed since our trek across Tibet. I failed, initially, to recognize this gaunt and grey facsimile of Charly, the clothes hanging off his emaciated body. He'd even shaved off his beard. Encountering him was the last thing on my mind; I'd safely assumed he'd be in Australia by now. Some degree of shock must have registered on my face.

"*Mon brave!* We meet again. Zis time eet is me who needs ze medication." He went on to explain that, shortly after we'd parted ways in Chengdu, he'd been hit by hepatitis. "I was in a coma for three weeks in Dali. Eet was a few months before I could move again. I just arrived on ze train from Guangzhou to 'Ong Kong, *et voila!*" His desire to get to Australia, once interrupted, was more urgent than ever, "Eet is ze land of opportunity, believe me. Don't waste your time 'ere."

We all needed a dream, something to keep us moving forward.

BUREAUCRAZY

"I GUESS WE should inform the authorities we have arrived," winced Pascal, sipping at his breakfast coffee on the sailing club veranda, disgusted by the thought of bureaucracy before the process even began.

"It would be nice not to ..." wished Fredy. But dive back into the real world we must, at some point. There had been no passport control at the sailing club, an astonishing loophole, when you thought about it. Monitoring of our movements, on land and by air, grows ever more severe and intrusive. Travel by sea however — no faster now than back in the day of Conrad's *Lord Jim* — and the world simply forgets you exist. Our motley gang of sunburnt and blistered buccaneers — dressed, uncomfortably now, in clothes — were unregistered aliens drifting through this glistening, high-tech, high-rise metropolis. We occupied two rows of seats at the front of the top deck of the No.2 bus from Changi Village to New Bridge Road, shattering local decorum with our spicy, wind-hardened chatter, still shouting orders across a swaying deck. Objective: the immigration office at Finger Pier. Below us Singapore flashed by, instantly familiar, yet tropically exotic. The Singapore Air Force holiday bungalows and former

RAF hospital where my ex-dispatch riding best friend Mark had been born — his father being in the air force and posted to the Far East at the time — next, the Lion City's feared Changi Prison; and everywhere, hedgerows of rhododendron, burning red hibiscus flowers and lazy palm trees.

We discovered the paradise of Little India, and the piquant perfection of South Indian cuisine at the *Sri Krishna* restaurant; elongated *masaladosas* with their various curries and sauces, washed down by Horlicks, providing multicultural harmony for the taste buds. Wandering from Dhoby Ghaut to Somerset we swayed and bumped into each other, as yet unused to the fixed horizon. We passed spellbound by Aladdin's cave electronic stores, filled-to-bursting supermarkets, and the open-air food centers of Orchard Road. I splashed out on a pair of boating shoes, but couldn't get used to wearing socks after running around for a fortnight barefooted on *Kurnia Ilahi*. As afternoon heated-up, I dropped off my slide films to be processed.

Almost as an after-thought we dropped in to the Immigration office and let them know the boys from *Kurnia Ilahi* were in town.

A day or two later I moved into the city, needing to be in a French-free zone for a while. The previous day had been mostly wasted on red tape. I was first in to the Indonesian Embassy when they opened. Explaining to the woman at front desk the circumstances that left me now requiring an Exit Visa from her country, she was full of sympathy but short on solutions to my dilemma and directed me to the man at counter 2. He heard me out, slightly less patiently, and then passed me on to his colleague at counter 4. My story was benefitting tremendously from all this retelling; in fact it was evolving into quite a saga. Counter 4 filled out a form and told me to go wait in the common area.

So far, so good. I had all the time in the world. I was full of hope for a swift, logical resolution to what, after all, was merely a minor and unintentional infringement of ill-defined regulation. After twenty minutes or so, I was called through to an office behind the row of counters, and from there shown into a smaller, windowless room. Here I awaited the next link in the bureaucratic chain. In strode a stocky employee with sweating brow, who slumped into a revolving chair and, ignoring me, made several phone calls whilst all the time chain smoking.

"I don't know why you were brought into this office," he eventually illuminated, and then set off for another meeting, instructing me only to, "Wait in the hallway."

I did as instructed, on my angelic best behavior. I was plied with glasses of sweet black coffee—the grinds sticking to the rim—and told to wait back in the reception area by the staff as they decamped for lunch. They kept my passport though; a promising hint at progress. At 2 p.m. I was escorted back into the inner sanctum where Fat Man was back, probing the gaps between his teeth with a bamboo toothpick. He was not at all happy with my story.

"You have no exit stamp from the port in Maumere," he shook his head at this grievous breach of protocol. "This is a most serious case. Most serious indeed." He seemed very curious about Pascal, and over coffee, relented a little. Pascal, I offered—sure in the knowledge our capitaine was flying to Paris tonight, and thus safe from the wrath of the Indonesian diplomatic corps—*did* have a passenger manifest, one that I had, in fact, witnessed being painstakingly typed out by "Rambo" Hussein, back on Jampea.

"Bring me this, and I will see what I can do."

The problem was now to catch a bus to Changi in time to intercept Pascal before his flight. I had in my pocket just 37 cents in cash, and there were no banks in this leafy, diplomatic district.

Fortunately, the British High Commission wasn't far. I ran the distance in ten minutes. The attractive Chinese Singaporean girl at the info counter sized up both my situation and me, immediately, telling me of the speediest bus route back out to Changi, and lending me a dollar for the fare.

I bumped into Franck at the CSC clubhouse. He told me I'd just missed Pascal. Luckily, he'd left the crew manifest with Xavier. Gilles was in a generous mood, shouting us all beers.

"Nice ... er ... *ladies* I saw you with the other night." I ventured, receiving a slightly chastened grin in reply.

"I thought so, too," admitted the ex-customs officer. "They were all over me at the food center in Changi Village and I thought to myself, Gilles, you are in luck. Of course, I had been drinking quite heavily beforehand."

"Ahh," I responded, in sympathy.

"There is nowhere for us to go, so I say 'come back to my boat' ... I guess they are all expecting a modern yacht. Well, they were most disappointed when we arrived." He took a sip from his can of Tiger Beer. "But not as disappointed as I was when I found out they were all lady-boys."

"Ahh," I repeated, marveling at the matter-of-fact way the French deal with these most delicate aspects of human nature. "So, you comforted each other in your mutual disappointment then ..."

"*Oui*, yes, it seemed the practical thing to do, since they were already on board. And they had such lovely legs ..."

The following day I headed back to the British High Commission to repay my debt, leaving an envelope containing two Singapore dollars in it at the front desk, marked:

To: The pretty young lady with long dark hair (sorry, I never

got your name) – Information Office, Brit. High Comm. etc.
"So, you're back," she looked up and smiled on seeing the envelope, "I work front desk Thursdays and Fridays."

"Ahh, yes, I see." I wished I could be suave like the French in situations like this. Instead, English embarrassment spread red across my face. "I don't suppose I could get a copy of this?" I changed subject, slipping her the crew manifest under the glass window.

"We're not allowed to make photocopies for the public ... *but since it's you.*"

Ready to do battle, I marched in to the Indonesian Embassy. But my efforts at flattery, apology, cajoling – indeed, anything short of pistol-whipping or bribery – failed to secure an Exit Visa. Not so very long ago, an Englishman could travel the globe without a passport, his word as his bond. But the modern world is a paranoid and petty place. Authority is blind: it fails to distinguish between the honest intentions of the gentleman adventurer, and the conniving of the criminally minded. Anyone who dares step out of the ordinary is tarred with the stinking brush of suspicion. I momentarily considered not returning to Indonesia at all. After all, talk around the lounge at the hostel was filled with possibilities for working in Thailand, and Japan. But my back was up: this was a challenge.

Orchard Road offered a necessary distraction. I picked up my slides from the lab in *Orchard Plaza*. The shots, somewhat surprisingly, had turned out very well. The slow, polychromatic slide film had soaked up the brilliant, tropical blues and reds of our passage in thick, saturated emulsion. Seeing my images reproduced on celluloid, in positive form, gave me *just* the confidence I needed.

Back at Sim's guesthouse, its avuncular owner Mr. Sim was

berating another clueless traveler with his catch phrase: 'Any more questions?' It was a homely dive, costing around US$2 a night for a bunk bed in an airy dormitory, and attracting an eclectic crowd of impoverished wastrels similar to myself. Lorne, a longhaired harmonica player from Camden Town, for instance, had been to Indonesia three times, already.

"You should meet my friend Jez, in Jakarta," he reviewed my sheets of slides, "I reckon you've got a story here; he's a photographer and will know someone in the magazines."

"Only problem is my lack of an exit visa," I told him, scraping out the daily reservoir of pus from my infected shin. I'd damaged it early on in the voyage, and no matter what creams, salves or sprays I used now, it kept on filling up and erupting, like a volcano.

"Why don't you come with me? I'm going back there next week. We can take the hydrofoil to Batam together," Lorne suggested. That Indonesian island lay just twenty miles from Singapore. It seemed crazy, almost disrespectful, to think that we could cross in just half-an-hour the same choppy and dangerous channels of the Singapore Strait it had taken us all night to conquer on *Kurnia Ilahi*.

One man's adventure is just another's daily commute.

"Worst case," Lorne continued, "they'll turn you back and you've wasted the return ferry fare. But at least you'll have tried." He looked down and winced involuntarily on catching sight of the discolored bandage wrapped around my left leg. This seemed to prompt in him the same fond and dreamy recollection I'd last witnessed in Charly when he enlightened me about the range of drugs on offer in Kathmandu: "Oh, and you can buy all kinds of shit over the counter at the chemists in Jakarta!"

That does it. I'm going back to Indonesia.

POSTE RESTANTE

I HAVE ALWAYS loved post offices: the grander the better. And you couldn't get much glitzier than Singapore's General Post Office. No lesser scribe than Joseph Conrad — writing of the earlier GPO here, one that had been demolished to make way for the present Fullerton building post office constructed in the mid-1920s — described it as 'the most important post office in the East'. Its location near the Lion City's symbolic water-spewing 'Merlion' statue, on the edge of Marina Bay, along with its imposing, colonnaded façade, led it to be known as the 'Grand Old Dame'.

I entered the lofty corridors, my eyes adjusting slowly to the deep shade within, feeling the sweat evaporate off me in air stirred slowly from above by ancient ceiling fans. Eager for news of anything from the outside world, I tracked down the *Poste Restante* counter. An official there pulled out three elongated wooden filing trays, each stuffed full with letters and aerogrammes placed in alphabetical order. I began to sift through this treasure, looking out for the names of friends I'd come across in my travels — trying to get some indication as to who may be in town at the moment — and for mine, in particular. First I checked under the initial of my surname. Nothing. Next, I pawed through the letters on either side of it, in case of clerical malfunction, and then I started on the 'Cs'. It was here I found the letter with West German stamps on it, and postmarked 'Bonn'. It had been sitting there, anticipating my arrival, for two months.

> *Leibe Chris,*
>
> *Can I be so presumptuous as to ever call you either 'idiot', or 'boy', again? After all, it seems so long since we met in Lhasa, and perhaps you are not now so unworldly or naïve, and with many new experiences under your belt. Part of me hopes you will not have changed too much – that is a selfish expectation, ignore it – since innocence is such a precious and delicate possession. But holding on to a little of it can help you sometimes see straight in this crazy world.*
>
> *You will notice this letter is a photocopy. You were rather vague in your last letter from Brisbane about your future travel plans. I got the impression you had sort of stalled in Australia and needed some inspiration and adventure to jolt you back into life again and give you direction. Accordingly, I have posted this same letter to the main post offices of all the major Asian capitals, from Jakarta to Bangkok. One of them will find you, I am sure of it!*

Well, I'd found that adventure, and then some! Claudia was a mind reader. I wasn't so sure about the direction side of things, though. Maybe something would come of my photos? It was a slender hope, but it was all I had to put my faith in.

Obviously the envelope I had entrusted to Gaby hadn't made it from Maumere to Europe yet. Now I think about it, what was I ever doing expecting him to honor his end of that deal? The letter currently bobbing in its bottle across the Indian Ocean probably stood a better chance of making its way into Claudia's hands first ...

*Enjoy your freedom my dear, it is a precarious substance.
We humans are no better than that dog running in endless
circles after its own tail. Maybe you, too, won't know
what to do with it, if ever you manage to catch hold of it?
That is not the best analogy, I know, but then English is
not my first language. I just mean to say we have precious
few chances to start life anew. Do not be too hasty to give
yourself up to routine or to listen to the advice of others –
apart from mine, of course – and always, always, watch out
for strange German girls wishing to take advantage of you
in sandstorms.*

Deine Claudia X

Was it me she was advising, or was the letter expressing some
inner regret about the progress of her own love life? I exited
the post office feeling oddly elated: Claudia still cared for me;
she cared enough to set me free. Not even the blinding and
oppressively hot midday sun, or liquid wall of tropical heat,
could dampen my mood.

BUGIS NIGHT

WE HAD BEEN in Singapore a week already. Franck, Gilles, Bruno and Xavier were still living aboard *Kurnia Ilahi*, out in Changi. Tonight, though, they had promised to bus in to the city in order for us to celebrate our nautical Rite of Passage, in Bugis Street. I couldn't imagine a scene further removed from the sober tranquility of Jampea island, whose sea-trading denizens originally lent their name to this infamous Singaporean enclave. But how could we possibly complete our journey together anywhere else?

Until a few years ago, drunken sailors flocked here to consecrate their maiden voyage to Singapore performing the 'Dance of the Flaming Arseholes' atop the public toilets on Malabar Street. Trousers around their ankles, a rolled-up newspaper blazing between clenched buttocks, the bravest seaman was judged the one who could stand the heat the longest. Packed lanes all about thronged and throbbed with transvestites, pimps, their customers and some gob-smacked (and quite possibly lost) tourists; all reveling until disbursed by the first rays of dawn.

It was perhaps fortunate, considering how many bottles of Tiger Beer laid now empty on our table, and how animated we had become, that opportunities for such abandoned exuberance had recently been reined-in. 'Bugis Street' was being gentrified and sanitized, made into a mall—a *destination*—even given its own Metro station, for God's sake. The wild party boat had sailed, leaving Gilles, in light of his recent Changi Village conquests, feeling cheated.

In consolation, we dined extravagantly. We proposed far too many toasts, and made rash promises to meet up for future adventures. A sudden gust encircled us, sending beer cans clattering along the pavement. Gripping the edge of the table, I leant back in my plastic stool and gazed up at the reflected ocean of stars above. Which of these shone the way back to Jampea island? I closed my eyes, letting the breeze wash over me like sea spray, and was clinging to the prow of *Kurnia Ilahi* once more.

Let go, my heart urged. Dive forever in the depths of this Bugis night.

AFTERMATH. AND ANOTHER
NEW BEGINNING

A Letter from the Editor

Compass Publishing, Singapore

To: Chris S.
C/o Poste Restante, GPO, Kuala Lumpur
27th November 1988

Dear Chris,
Thank you for your submission to *South East Asia Traveller*, it was a pleasure to meet in our office yesterday. We do have a special Adventure Issue coming up shortly, and I think your story very suitable to include in this.

Since I would like to feature your marvelous photographs, would it be possible to edit your text down to 1,800 words, whilst keeping the 'feeling' the same, and pop that revised text in the post by, say, January?

All the best
Anna
Anna Juliet Ross - Editor, S.E.A. Traveller

THE FATE OF *KURNIA ILAHI*

Penang, Malaysia
December 1988

"HI, I'M MAGNUS." The tall, slim boy with mop of curly blond hair dropped his pack in the dormitory.

At first, I thought it must be Fredy, playing a trick. But Fredy was long gone. He'd skipped Singapore — and Pascal — as quick as he could, back to Indonesia with a fresh visa, intent on completing his interrupted journey to Australia. I hoped he'd write, though suspected he was not the type to dwell on the past.

"From Sweden," Magnus shattered my reverie.

"Chris. England. Have a seat."

"Odd that it is Christmas, and no snow," Magnus lamented before laughing, "Well, not odd for the Malays, I guess. You know what I mean?"

"It's my second winter away. I spent the last one in Australia. No snow there, either. Seasons all upside down." We engaged in familiar backpacker one-upmanship; a crude hierarchy of experience established by dint of length of time spent away from home, number of countries visited and types of exotic illnesses suffered. I kept my trump card, the voyage on *Kurnia Ilahi*, as an ace up my sleeve.

"I just arrived from India," lamented Magnus, "been shitting like a monsoon drain ever since a dodgy dal in Darjeeling."

It was amazing how open you could be with people you knew you'd never see again after tomorrow. His face bore a pinched and pensive look, and I was sure he was about to excuse himself and make a dash for the loo. Instead, he swallowed an Imodium tablet, as though readying himself for battle: "Yes, I didn't expect to travel to India at all. Sort of washed up there with no visa."

"That sounds rather careless of you," I said, secretly impressed.

"Well, I'd been on a boat, you see. We sailed out of Singapore and through the Strait of Malacca. We managed to avoid all the pirates there, and were all feeling rather pleased with ourselves, when the boom goes and snaps in the middle."

Hearing this, a stone sank in my stomach. I recalled distinctly the sound a snapping bamboo boom made — like a gunshot fired at close range. But surely modern-day yacht booms were made of aluminum?

"A little while later, the rudder snaps in two and we start drifting out into the Indian Ocean, next stop: Madagascar!"

"Hell! Couldn't you use your engine, or radio for assistance?" I asked, my heart pounding as I remembered being in a similar fix not so long ago on *Kurnia Ilahi*.

"It wasn't that kind of boat. It was a Bugis ship, made entirely of wood. They were trying to sail it to France, but they were woefully under equipped and the Captain,"

"... Pascal!" I finished his sentence.

"What?" Magnus almost jumped out of his chair. "How on earth do you know about him?" And I recounted the tale of our voyage, of meeting Pascal and the others in Maumere, of Jampea, and of the storm.

"So, you are *that* Chris!" Magnus soon made the connection. "Gilles mentioned you a lot." Franck, Magnus informed me, had not set sail from Singapore, preferring instead to explore a bit of Malaysia first, He had waited for weeks, right here in Penang, expecting any day to be picked up by *Kurnia Ilahi* when Pascal and the others pulled in for supplies, and pick up the adventure from there. But our Bugis Lady never arrived.

"Whatever happened? How on earth did you manage to sail to India with a broken rudder?" I wondered, incredulous at such a feat, almost wishing I'd been along for the adventure, too.

"But we didn't sail to India. Well, not on *Kurnia Ilahi*, anyway," said Magnus, his expression suddenly turning serious: "You know how Pascal was always saying they should re-caulk the hull? Well, that never got done, obviously. So, we are not only drifting but taking on loads of water, too; *Kurnia* is slowly sinking. Luckily Bruno, or one of them, had picked up some distress flares in Singapore. We fired them all off at night and were spotted by the *Albertstadt*, an East German cargo ship. It rescued us as waves were beginning to lap our feet, and dropped us off in Calcutta four days later!"

By now it was late. Magnus and I, wary of our loquacious chatter keeping the other occupants of the dormitory awake, headed down to Love Lane, the main hostel street below. Here we found a roadside coffee shop where elderly Chinese sat on plastic stools smoking and playing mahjong under flickering fluorescent strips. I bought a round of ABC Stout, the only beer they stocked. The cans dripped as the owner scooped them from a bucket of icy water and brought them to our table. I snapped mine open, hoping the metallic fizz would jolt Magnus into continuing his tale, but he was hesitating, as though fighting back some unpleasant truth that he knew must come out.

"It was Pascal's idea: *We can't leave the ship out here just below the surface, she will be a danger to shipping.* You know how his word is final ..."

"And so?" I prompted. Magnus swigged back his beer and looked me in the eye.

"And so, with the cargo ship approaching, he took an axe and smashed a great hole in her hull. Still *Kurnia* won't sink, well, not immediately. She is made out of wood, after all. When I think about that tough little boat, well, *you* know what I mean, more than anyone!"

Yes, I do, Magnus. I really do. I pretended to be wiping sweat from my face, but it was tears that were welling up inside me. Tears of pride and exhaustion, great salty drops of ocean dew that could no longer be held back as I pictured of our brave little ship, battling against such odds to deliver us safely to Singapore; tears of relief and of loss and of love for *Kurnia Ilahi*.

We continued to drink. That subtle watershed — the one that lay between sensibly calling it a night, and forging recklessly on — had come and gone a few cans back. Neither Magnus nor I felt it passing. And the café owner seemed happy enough to keep the place open and indulge our weakness.

"Don't look behind you," Magnus warned suddenly, "but there is someone in that group over there who has been staring at you, for ages."

"What, some drunk?" I sat up a little straighter, wiping my face dry with my neck scarf, and cleared my mental deck for confrontation. I chose to stay seated, though, rather than expose my degree of intoxication, on unsteady legs.

"Well, they're drinking, but seem normal enough. Hang on, one of them is coming over here ..."

Magnus looked beyond me, over my shoulder, his head angling upwards as one from the group approached our table.

The hairs on my neck tingled with nervous static ... and then I picked up the faintest scent of honey and wildflowers mingling with the cigarette smoke. Before I could turn on my stool a body had launched itself at me, and I was being held in a strong embrace:

"It *is* you! Why did you shave your beard off? I hardly recognized you, idiot boy!" grinned Claudia.

JAKARTA, FOR NOW ...

WE'RE HEADING BACK on a PELNI ship to Jakarta, it's where I live now, and teach English (though I hope not to teach for much longer). Claudia has a month off from her new job and we're planning to use it, doing the things normal tourists do, like visit Bali and sit on beaches and ... well, I have no idea what else tourists fill their time with ... perhaps we'll get to follow in Charly's footsteps, and 'climb Kelimutu'?

I write a note explaining the poignant fate of *Kurnia Ilahi*, and post it to Anna, the magazine editor in Singapore who is considering running my story of the voyage.

I'll believe *that* when I see it in print.

Before sealing the envelope and heading down to the post office, I remember to add the words a wise Bugis sailor once told me about his ship: "*She knows how to get home on her own. All I do is hang on to the tiller.*"

Compass Publishing, Singapore

To: Chris S.
C/o Peter Pan School of English, Jakarta
13th January 1989

Dear Chris,

Will wonders ever cease! I'm glad you weren't on the Kurnia Ilahi and had returned to Jakarta by passenger ship—not that old wreck!

Anyway, thanks for writing—your letter informing us of the fate of your ship caused no end of amazement/amusement.

Well, try not to get killed before you see your name in print!

All the best,

Anna

Anna Juliet Ross—Editor, S.E.A. Traveller

DISCLAIMER

I HAVE STRIVEN to portray conversations, people and their actions as recorded in the diary (no.14) I kept during the voyage, from saved letters and, where this has not been possible, then to the best of my memory and in the spirit of the moment. A couple of characters reside behind the protective wall of pseudonym, and a few episodes have been reframed or embellished – to greater or lesser degree – for the sake of dramatic effect. It has been a fortune of my life to have kept in touch with Franck Dubois who has been able to update me on the fate of our crew and give me the French take on some of the events described in these pages.

To those who lent me permission to use their real names and experiences go my heartfelt thanks. And to the many friends and acquaintances with whom I have lost contact over the course of half a lifetime, I can only hope that, if you come across this imperfect attempt to recreate the magical days of our youth, my story will bring a smile to your face, and you'll forgive me the rare flight of fancy.

ACKNOWLEDGEMENTS

For my Mother and Father, and my sister Jennie—who allowed me the freedom to travel, all those years ago—the greatest gift of all! To the crew of *Kurnia Ilahi*: Franck Dubois, Pascal Trouve, Fredy Ruhstaller and Xavier Aubry, Gilles-Marie Chenot (1963-2014) and Bruno Roussel (1965-1997). To Jana Steiger, eternal thanks for the countless conference calls half way around the world and late into the night as you helped me edit this draft into shape, and for keeping faith in the project even when I felt like giving in!

To Christiane Hammer (1956-2021), we'll always have Tibet. And to Charly Godin, Yee Wai-Fong and siblings, Anna Murphy (née Ross), Uli Neumann, Lorne Stockman and Jez O'Hare, and to Pak Sauda and any inhabitants of Jampea island who may recall a strange visitation, back in the September of 1988.

I am grateful to Captain Larry Heron for helping straighten out the nautical terminology; David Frazier for his expert editing guidance; Andy Jelfs for general support and encouragement from afar; and Don Shapiro, Keith Loveard, Alberto Buzzola, Hans Kemp, Reed Resnikoff, Paul Ehrlich, John Fowler, Al Reyes, Jeff Topping, Alan Sargent, Scott Weaver, Debbie Nock, Richard

CHRIS STOWERS

McCallum, Uval Daniel, Sinartus Sosrodjojo and Family, and Ralph Jennings—among many others—for variously reading through parts of the manuscript and/or offering advice and cheerleading beyond the call of duty.

A big nod to Gary Melyan for all the fine dining, and Jim Cumming and Paul Hu, for keeping the whisky flowing—all in the interests of creativity, of course. Finally, thanks to the ever-patient May Huang at *Sir Speedy* printers in Taipei for her tireless help with the manuscripts and mock-ups.

The author and our sampan at Changi Sailing Club circa 2010. The vessel was used as an ornamental flowerbed for more than 20 years after our arrival on Kurnia Ilahi, and may, possibly, still be found there today. Photo © YEE Wai-fun

ABOUT THE AUTHOR

The author is a professional photographer, based in Asia. He is represented by Panos Pictures photo agency in London, and has traveled, lived and worked in more than 70 countries since setting out from his native England, in 1987.

Despite multiple visits to Indonesia since the events portrayed in this book, he never did manage to find his way back to Jampea island ...

Ingram Content Group UK Ltd.
Milton Keynes UK
UKHW041052130723
424925UK00007B/68